Holy Together

Holy Together

Reflections on Married Spirituality

KATHLEEN FINLEY

RESOURCE *Publications* • Eugene, Oregon

HOLY TOGETHER
Reflections on Married Spirituality

Resource Publications
An Imprint of Wipf and Stock Publishers
199 W. 8th Ave., Suite 3
Eugene, OR 97401

www.wipfandstock.com

PAPERBACK ISBN: 978-1-7252-8448-7
HARDCOVER ISBN: 978-1-7252-8449-4
EBOOK ISBN: 978-1-7252-8450-0

Manufactured in the U.S.A.   08/31/20

Contents

Introduction

To BE MARRIED IS to be delighted at times, challenged at others, and to be immersed in deeply spiritual waters. Because this spirituality lies well disguised behind the everyday realities of our lives, it can take some exploring and reflecting for us to see it clearly for what it is: a place with deep potential for inner life and growth. Together we will explore some of what that spirituality looks like in an everyday, practical sense, not theoretically. (More about how I understand the word "spirituality" a little later here.)

HOW THIS BOOK CAME TO BE

This book had its beginnings in my desire to reflect on my own marriage and its spirituality as a surprise for my husband for our fortieth anniversary, which has now come and gone. You will find what I wrote for him in the Appendix here, but more about that later. Because I have had the privilege of working with engaged couples for over 25 years, as well as teaching about Christian Marriage and Christian Spirituality in a university setting for many years, I could see how much of what I was working with applied to our experience as a couple, and I wanted to explore it further.

That personal reflection, with terms from spirituality that I had been teaching about for many years, morphed into this examination of what is holy in any marriage. To do that I use seven concepts from Christian spirituality—grace, vocation, community, asceticism, incarnation, discernment, and dying and rising. I have explored each of them from a Catholic perspective, since that what I am, through and through. At the same time, most of what you'll find here is applicable to just about any spiritual tradition.

WHAT *IS* SPIRITUALITY?

Spirituality is a fairly recent term to describe how one lives out one's beliefs. Many have tried to define it, including the well-known spiritual writer Henri Nouwen who said that spirituality is the active presence of God in the midst of a life that is frequently preoccupied by worries and anxieties.

U Thant, the former Secretary-General of the United Nations, suggested that spirituality is the tuning in of the inner person to the great mysteries and secrets that are all around us.

Research professor and storyteller Brene Brown observed that spirituality is recognizing that we are all united by a power that connects us to one another, a power that is rooted in love and compassion. Practicing spirituality brings a sense of perspective, meaning, and purpose to our lives.

Benedictine monk Brother David Steindl-Rast said that sometimes people get the mistaken notion that spirituality is a separate department of life, the penthouse of existence. On the contrary, he declared, spirituality is a lively awareness that permeates and binds together all aspects of our existence.

To all this I would add my own rather simple definition: Spirituality is the way I live in light of what I believe. This spirituality, of course, happens in a specific culture, the influence of which we're not fully aware because it is "the water in which we swim." In the midst of a particular culture, if I believe as a Christian that Jesus was the Incarnation of God and died and rose, then my spirituality is Christian. For no other religion shares this belief.

WHAT ARE THESE SEVEN ASPECTS?

I mentioned seven concepts from the spiritual tradition that we will be exploring when it comes to the experience of marriage. Here they are:

- The foundational reality of any marriage as *grace* is a full, overwhelming sense of God's undeserved love in the midst of our powerful love for each other.

- The sense of *vocation*, of a call from God, is far more than something just for priests and nuns or anyone in formal ministry. Each couple, each family has a unique call to live out being a place where God's love is known and shared.

- Every couple and family is a *community* and has around them a community of support which, paradoxically, they need even more and yet may be less aware of while living in our strongly individualistic culture.

- In the course of any couple's life there is an ongoing need, at times, for each one to give up his or her own personal preferences and needs for the good of the couple, which is a kind of *asceticism*, a classic spiritual practice.

- Marriage is a place where spiritual experience exists in the midst of the daily and bodily realities of life, and that can help make it easier to understand both the *Incarnation*— God becoming flesh in Jesus— and thinking holistically.

- The web of choices that makes up a couple's life together is the result of careful decision-making and sometimes the use of *discernment*. Listening to the Spirit's presence in their lives, whether they're aware of doing so or not, can help deepen those choices.

- In the most difficult experiences that couples share, as well as in their daily lives, marriages experience the *dying and rising* that was part of Jesus' life, with new life emerging from those events in ways that they never could have imagined.

HOW WE WILL EXPLORE THESE IDEAS

Because each of these seven concepts may not be familiar or easy to understand in the context of marriage, we will first clarify what each one is and is not by briefly examining a couple of models or guides in the Christian spiritual tradition, models who embody this concept. These saints or saint-like figures, by their lives and their words, will help us understand what we will then explore in the experience of marriage.

We will examine one particular couple's encounter with each of these seven concepts and discuss some of the various elements within it. At the end of each chapter you'll find some reflection questions for individuals and couples to consider; these could also be used in a small group setting for faith sharing. Finally, you'll see a brief passage from Scripture to connect our reflection to the biblical tradition and also a list of books which may be helpful if you wish to explore the issue further. You'll notice that not all the resources listed are explicitly religious in nature because spirituality connects with a variety of disciplines, including psychology and counseling.

In the Appendix I've included what I first wrote to my husband Mitch to help show what it might look like to apply these categories to a particular marriage. Our marriage isn't typical in some ways, because of our academic theological background, and it certainly isn't perfect. I include that section to encourage readers to apply these concepts to their own marital history.

CHALLENGING *AND* HOLY

As we live in a world that daily becomes more complex and challenging, we desperately need to reflect on how to love well and faithfully. We see plenty of examples around us of how to do marriage poorly, with plenty of selfishness and what's-in-it-for-me, along with manipulation and trying to make ourselves look good instead of focusing on each other. Many of us also unintentionally transfer woundedness from our past into our marriages, confusing the past with the present. The problem is that we don't want love to cost as much as we find that it does, and it's harder than we thought to put in the work required. But it's well worth the effort in the end. And it is, indeed, holy. The Trappist monk and author Thomas Merton once observed that life is actually quite simple. We live, he said, in a world that is utterly transparent with God beaming through it constantly. At the same time, we won't see the divine presence unless we give ourselves up to God's love; but when we do we will see the God who is absolute love shining through in everything—including people, things, happenings and the natural world. In truth, Merton said, God is everywhere at all times, and we can't continue to exist without his love. What gets in the way of our seeing this and makes our lives opaque rather than transparent, Merton suggests, is our concerns and worries, day in and day out.

As we explore together the ways that marriage can be transparent at times, we'll see that a couple's life is often holier—more drenched in the presence of God—than they may have imagined. As we do so, my hope is that you may be like the Old Testament figure Jacob, who has a consoling dream of a stairway and path to heaven and of God's faithful presence. Perhaps, with him, you will be able to look again at your own marriage and home and say, "Truly, the Lord is in this spot, although I did not know it" (Genesis 28:17)!

Chapter One

Love Outpoured

Grace in Our Marriage

IN ORDER TO UNDERSTAND grace, God's loving presence in our lives, we first turn to two unlikely and seemingly unremarkable people who lived many centuries ago, hidden away by choice from the mainstream of life .

OUR GUIDES: JULIAN OF NORWICH AND BROTHER LAWRENCE

The first person we know as Julian of Norwich. Actually, we don't know her real name because she took on the name of the church of St. Julian where she was an anchoress, a woman who for religious reasons withdrew from ordinary, everyday life to embrace a life of prayer. She lived much of her life enclosed in her small room, attached to the church in Norwich, England. From there she was able to be a source of spiritual help and reassurance to those who came to her in the 14th and early 15th centuries. This was a time of considerable turmoil, with issues such as the Black Plague, wars, and other problems. What would someone with such a different life from ours have to teach us about God's grace? Plenty, it turns out.

Once when she was severely ill Julian experienced God's presence powerfully in what she called "showings," visions which she wrote down later in the first book known to be authored by a woman in English. She talked about God's love and grace in a way quite striking, for this was a time

1

when the popular focus was on God's wrath and punishment for sin. Julian wrote that because God's tender love embraces all, God quickly comforts those who turn to him. Julian famously wrote that God said to her, "All shall be well, and all shall be well, and all manner of thing shall be well."

Julian's images were familiar and vivid. She wrote that God showed her a little thing no bigger than a hazelnut. Julian explained that she looked at it and thought, 'What can it be?' Then she received the answer, "It is all that is made." Astonished, she wondered how such a little thing could could survive. Then into her mind came the answer that it survives and will always do so because God loves it. In other words, Julian realized that even such a little thing receives its being from God's love.

As she spoke about the love of God, Julian did something truly amazing for her time: she referred to God not just as Father but as a tender Mother also. It dawned on Julian that God gives us, free and undeserved, the grace to respond to the invitation to become children of God and to share in the divine nature and in eternal life.

In the face of this free and undeserved help, this grace that Julian described, what is our response? We are called to stay open to God's love, to abide in and bask in it. But how do we do this? We may find help from a humble cook in a seventeenth-century Carmelite monastery.

Brother Lawrence was a simple man, perhaps wounded in battle before he entered a monastery in France as a lay brother. He was not ordained as a priest but lived a life of prayer and service, and he worked in the monastery kitchen for some forty years. A visitor there, who happened to be on the staff of the Cardinal of Paris, discovered in conversation with this simple brother the depth of his spiritual wisdom. The visitor later helped record Lawrence's simple yet profound approach to how to draw near to God and God's grace.

Brother Lawrence explained that the most holy practice, and the one most essential for the spiritual life, is to cultivate an awareness of the presence of God. He described how to find joy in God's divine company and to make it a habit to speak humbly and talk lovingly with God at all times, every moment of the day.

Brother Lawrence's approach was simple and commonsense. He explained that one need not be in church to be close to God, that God is always there with us and that it's only a matter of turning to God at various times in our day, whatever we are doing. That can apply whether among the pots and pans like Brother Lawrence or today at the computer or wherever we may be.

Both Julian of Norwich and Brother Lawrence remind us that God's love and grace are always there, waiting for us to discover and tune into it. Let's see next how grace takes shape in the spirituality of marriage.

GREG AND ANNE

Greg was there to visit Anne, day after day, week after week, for more months and years than the staff at the care facility could remember, even though because of her dementia his wife hadn't shown any sign of recognition of him for a long time. When he was asked why he kept coming every day, even when she didn't know who he was, his answer was, "Because I know who *I* am." Just as simple as that.

Greg's love for Anne is faithful—more than most of us will ever be called to be—and he is living out his vow for better or for worse. His constancy may even be a response to his own loneliness. But there's something more here; Greg reflects and lives out the grace that God gives him and each of us, a love that takes our breath away with its complete enfolding of all that we are—our mistakes, faults and even sins—a love that loves with no conditions and no possible way for us to earn that love.

A COMPLETE GIFT

Often, when we least expect it, we see the kind of love that Greg shows, a love that never gives up and that knows us through and through and still loves what it sees. Franciscan Fr. Richard Rohr says that God loves us not because we are good but because God is good. The bad news—and also the good news—is that there is nothing we can do to earn God's love.

The spiritual writer Frederick Buechner explains it this way: The grace of God means something like this: Here is your life. You might never have existed, but you *are* because it wouldn't have been the same without you. Yes, and here is the world. Beautiful and terrible things may and do happen. All the same, do not be afraid. God's love is with you. Nothing can ever separate you from God. In fact, God created the universe for you, and he loves you.

It's the *complete gift* of this love that is hard for us to wrap our heads and hearts around, since we live in a world that is so focused on a merit-based way of thinking, an approach that says I worked and/or studied hard to get this position, this raise, this house, and so I deserve it.

When I first learned about grace in catechism class many years ago, it was presented as something that I could get more of from certain sacraments and with certain actions. Grace is certainly there in each sacrament, but now I think about grace as the love of God *that breaks every rule and every expectation we have of God,* that is embarrassingly generous and always delights in us and is ready to take us back whenever we are willing to turn toward God.

This grace is clearly there in the promise of a marriage: My spouse knows me better than I know myself and sees things in me that others cannot see, things even *I* cannot see. My spouse can encourage me to become my best self. My spouse knows me to my very heart and loves what he or she sees! The experience of being in love can seem so impossible to us until we're in the midst of it. Grace in marriage is about far more than the wedding. That ceremony is a mere taste of what we've already been experiencing in our relationship and what we will continue to plunge into more deeply as the years go by, a reality that takes one's breath away.

HOW WE MET

Even the story of how any couple met is invariably a story of grace, no matter how it happened. Perhaps we grew up together and gradually noticed the energy from the other or maybe there was an unexpected meeting—perhaps online or in person—or anything in between.

Through many years of helping engaged couples prepare for marriage I've heard some incredible stories of how they met. Sometimes in retrospect the tale can seem like repeated attempts on God's part to bring a couple together, attempts that were finally successful.

When my husband and I met, we were in our mid-twenties and had almost no experience of dating, with little thought of meeting someone with whom to share our lives. We were at a meeting of parish directors of religious education and found that we had an amazing amount in common. Within six months we were married!

Think about the story of how the two of you met and see it again as strong evidence for the grace that was there at the beginning of your relationship, drawing you closer to each other and to God's tender and relentless love.

OUR SENSE OF SELF

Unfortunately, most of us bring into our marriage fears and filters that can cloud this grace we have been discussing. This may include a sense of myself that is uncertain at best, not ready to believe that I am really lovable and worthy of the grace of my spouse's love. The reasons, of course, are many. They range from the ragged give-and-take with siblings and peers when we were growing up to parental neglect and/or abuse, whether emotional, physical, or verbal.

Media influences can also be insidious.Thanks to advertising in many formats, we are presented with an array of impossible standards, physically and socially. We are told, for example, that our teeth aren't white enough, that our breath isn't as fresh, or our hair isn't as attractive as it could be. We *must* buy this toothpaste, this breath mint or shampoo to improve ourselves. While the goal of a commercial is to sell a product, the impression we come away with is that we just don't measure up to what we should be. This, in turn, makes it difficult for us to hear the kind of love and grace that waits patiently for us.

Our love history can be another negative filter; I first heard the phrase "loving with a limp" many years ago and thought it was a great image for the ways that our past hurts and wounds in love can make us reluctant to trust again. As we begin to understand our past, we can see the ways in which our little, or not so little, disappointments changed us and how we were victimized by small or large injustices. We can work to name and confront those hurts in order to heal them, and this can make a big difference in our ability to be open to love's invitation to grace. Otherwise, there may be energy stuck somewhere in our past that doesn't allow our full selves to be present to a current relationship and its promise.

As I begin to know myself and the me that I bring to a relationship, I can begin to see not only my strengths but also my weaknesses and faults. And, perhaps, I may discover that those strengths and failings are not far from each other, after all; it's a question of balance. For example, if I'm a good detail person and a planner—by nature or because of a job or other position of responsibility—when that same quality is out of balance, it can lead to being too picky and to being a perfectionist. An easygoing person, when out of balance, can be too easily manipulated or perhaps be oblivious to others' feelings. A natural people-helper can easily get caught up in others and their needs and overlook good self-care. In each case, it's the same quality; the question is whether or not it's in a healthy balance.

DIFFERENCES IN OUR BACKGROUNDS

Yet another challenge that we bring to a relationship, and the grace waiting there, is our cultural or ethnic differences, or perhaps a disparity in our economic or educational backgrounds. As we first get to know each other we're often convinced that our love will conquer any differences between us, but as time goes on those parts of our backgrounds can loom as far more powerful than we could have imagined. We'll explore this further when we consider how community affects our spirituality.

UNDERSTANDING WHAT LOVE IS—AND ISN'T

We bring some powerful beliefs about what love is and is not to our experience of grace with another. We're learning more all the time about how individuals learn to love and to accept the grace that is offered there. For example, we now better understand the importance of secure infant and early childhood attachment to a caregiver. When that strong connection was not a part of our earliest experience it can affect us deeply as adults. We may want others close, and yet we also are afraid to let them get too close. This dynamic for couples is explored quite effectively in Emotionally Focused Therapy (EFT) and in books like *Hold Me Tight*, by Dr. Sue Johnson.

On the other hand, there are plenty of inaccurate and conditional ideas of love that we can accept too easily. I may think of love as being in control ("If you love me you will do what I want.") or love as agreement ("If you love me you will always see things the way I do."). Or perhaps I see love as understanding ("If you love me you will always know what I need or want without my having to say so.") or as conformity and obligation ("If you love me you will fit with me and all our friends and owe me your loyalty."). These incomplete notions of love can get in the way of accepting and being open to the grace of the other's love. (I go into these further in my book *Building a Christian Marriage: Eleven Essential Skills*.)

Besides learning about love in general from our experience, we also pick up more than we know from the couples we observe around us. When I'm helping prepare engaged couples for marriage, I ask each person about the most admirable marriage relationship they have seen. I ask this because I want to see whether they've been able to see a healthy, working couple relationship up close so that they have a realistic picture in their heads of what a healthy marriage looks like and have some idea of what to aim for in their own relationship. Some individuals haven't had that opportunity, and that can mean tolerating or overlooking behavior that they don't recognize as unhealthy.

THE RISK OF VULNERABILITY: NO GUARANTEES

Although we may try to be as open as possible to the love and grace of the other person, the reality is that as the years pass this openness can fade. What happens to dull our ability to stay open and grow closer to each other?

When we're really honest with ourselves, a key reason is that it's hard work to stay close to the other person, and there are no guarantees. How do I know that you will accept me as I open myself further to you and not laugh in my face this time—perhaps as others have done in the past, which may have led to my loving with a limp? In *Why Am I Afraid to Tell You Who I Am?* author John Powell wisely observed that if I tell you who I really am, you may not like who I am. But this is who I am, and it's all that I have.

No matter how long we're together and how much I know and trust your love, there is still a part of me that may be uncertain that *this time* you will accept me as I am. I may be uncertain that God's grace at the heart of our love will accept me this time, too. In her book *Daring Greatly: How the Courage to Be Vulnerable Transforms the Way We Live, Love, Parent and Lead* and also in her TED talks researcher Brene Brown discusses the implications of our reluctance to risk. When we give in to fear and find ourselves becoming numb toward another to reduce the risk, it changes everything: She says that becoming insensitive toward the other does not merely deaden the pain of difficult experiences; it also dulls our experiences of love, joy, belonging, creativity, and empathy. In other words, if we choose to numb unpleasant feelings we will find ourselves growing numb to positive feelings, too. Numb the dark and you numb the light, as well.

One related and powerful way that we try to duck the invitation of grace and its freedom is addiction in its various forms. In his book *Addiction and Grace* psychiatrist Gerald May says that all of us suffer from addictions that force us to worship these attachments instead of God. He says that addiction weakens the energy of our deepest desire to be loving and good. Whether it's the more commonly recognized addictions like alcohol or other drugs or an addiction to shopping, gambling or to the technology that constantly surrounds us or even always being right, there are plenty of things that can sidetrack our attention and ability to be open to love and grace. We would all do well to learn about the twelve steps of Alcoholics Anonymous and its related groups to realize that we are all powerless before these addictions without our "Higher Power," God's amazing gift of grace in our lives.

FORGIVENESS, A GIFT TO MYSELF

The sad reality is that at times we tend to avoid vulnerability and the grace of our love for each other, only to realize it later. For example, I may tell you a white lie when you ask if anything is wrong or how my day has been, or I may take you for granted or hide from fuller intimacy with you, substituting my job, or hobbies, or technology. (Usually it's much easier to see this in someone else than to see it in myself.)

When it becomes clear that this has happened again, we are each faced with a choice: do I admit that I haven't trusted you the way I know I can, and are you willing to forgive me? And can I forgive you for the ways that you have hurt me, even when you may not realize it or are not ready to acknowledge the situation?

The forgiveness between us—or lack of it—is directly connected to the grace and mercy that God shows each of us. If God forgives me so often and loves me so completely, warts and all, how can I love you any less? But if I forgive you—again—am I allowing you to "get away" with something that isn't okay? Am I enabling you to do the same thing again, asking for forgiveness again, over and over?

As we learn more about the process of authentic forgiveness, it is increasingly clear that when I forgive *you*, the one who really benefits is *me*. Whether or not you are ready to acknowledge the hurt in the situation, I no longer have to carry around as much resentment about what happened, and I'm more free to love you—and myself—more fully. Mike Leach, a wonderful writer, editor and friend, talks about marriage as not only a cosmic crapshoot but also a graduate school for mercy. You have to be lucky enough, he says, to marry the right person but then you must also *be* the right person, day in and day out. And, he continues, the miracle is this: when we are the right person but do the wrong thing, everything still turns out right.

THE LANGUAGES OF LOVE

When I want to express my love for you and the grace that is at the heart of it, how do I show how much I appreciate you? Gary Chapman in *The Five Love Languages* wisely points out that we don't all give or receive love in the same way. He identifies at least five different ways that we can express our love for another, and he says we each have a preferred style or two, which we often are not consciously aware of. My style may be *words of affirmation*, telling you how much you mean to me, or *quality time*, just being together, or *giving gifts*, sharing a token of how much you mean to me. Then again, it may mean that by *acts of service*, doing something around the house, or by *physical touch*, when just reaching for you, I show you how important you are. The trick of it is that our "love languages" are rarely exactly the same between spouses.

So what happens as a couple? Think of what happens when one spouse gets sick. Generally speaking, one person often likes to be taken care of and checked on when sick, and the other wants to be left alone until he or she feels better. If the leave-me-alone person is the one who's sick, the partner—who likes to be taken care of—will likely take care of the one who would just like to lay there. But if we reverse the picture and have the take-care-of-me partner get sick, he or she will often be left alone by the other partner because that's what that person would prefer for him- or herself! We tend to care for others the way we would like to be cared for, and that often happens with our preferred love language, as well.

Chapman suggests that to detect our preferred language of love we can watch for what annoys or hurts us, because that is when we experience the lack of what we want or need. We can also notice what we ask for from the other, like when I ask my spouse for praise after I work in the garden. Yet another clue can be what we offer to the other. For example, if I offer to rub your back, it may mean that is what I would like you to do for me.

However we give and receive love for each other, at the core of that love is a grace that is greater than we can begin to imagine or hope for. At the moments when we feel unworthy of the other's love we come close to sensing this reality.

SACRAMENT: GRACE AT THE CORE

We quickly come to a place of no words when we try to talk about God's love in the midst of our love. When my husband and I were engaged, there was no email. So, because we could only see each other on weekends we wrote letters almost daily to each other. In one of his letters, he wrote:

> I feel like maybe for the first time in my life—or at least in a completely new way—I know something of what "God" means, what "God" is all about. And all because of *you*. Because of *us*."

And later:

> Whenever I think of you or think of you thinking of me . . . *me!* Of all people! . . I rather quietly go bananas. A joy far beyond mere "whoopee," far deeper and more silent.

In their wise book *Marital Intimacy:A Catholic Perspective*, Joan Meyer Anzia and Mary G. Durkin discuss how marriage begins with falling in love: The other offers me a glimpse of the meaning of life. He or she becomes a sacrament, awakening me to the need to move outside of myself if I want to experience love. Falling in love is a deeply religious experience. We rediscover God's plan for creation. No wonder it is so wonderful. (More about this book later.)

The other *is* a sacrament for us, as the Catholic tradition wisely points out. If a sacrament is a visible, tangible sign of God's invisible, intangible love, then we might say that each of the seven sacraments of the Catholic tradition highlights one aspect of God's love: In Baptism we see God's *welcoming* love, welcoming an infant or older person into the community of believers to die and rise with Christ. In Confirmation we celebrate God's *strengthening* love offered through the Holy Spirit to live out this dying and rising. And in Eucharist we are given bread and wine, the body and blood—the whole person—of the risen Christ. This, in turn, *nourishes* us to *be* Christ in our time and place. Reconciliation offers us the *forgiving* love of God and the chance to forgive ourselves as God has already forgiven us. In Holy Orders we celebrate the *serving* love of Christ, a love that washes the disciples' feet at the Last Supper and invites us and those being ordained to do the same for one another. And in the Anointing of the Sick we celebrate God's *healing* love, hopefully a physical healing but also mending us spiritually from the isolation that illness of all kinds brings with it. Last but not least, Matrimony celebrates God's *lifelong commitment* never to give up on us. The couple promises the rest of their lives, not even knowing what the next minute, day or year will bring, based in turn on God's forever love for them.

Husband and wife are a visible, tangible sign of God's love in at least three ways: to each other, to others, and because of others. They are a sign of God's love *to each other*, day in and day out, of God's welcoming, strengthening, nourishing, forgiving, serving, healing and committed love. I tell engaged couples that the closest they'll ever get to God's love this side of the grave is the person sitting next to them right now. We are privileged to be a unique witness to each other's lives. And Matrimony is the only sacrament where the usual minister is not a priest or a deacon but the couple themselves.

Spouses are also a sign of God's love *to others* around them. From the time they are engaged and before, family and friends are watching how they are with each other, and since God is love, they are showing God to those others in their lives by their love for each other.

And they are a sign of God's love *because of others*. On their wedding day they can see before them most of the important people who have helped them to become who each of them is. They are ready to promise the rest of their lives, basing their "yes" to each other on so many yeses they have experienced in their lives so far.

❖ ❖ ❖

As we experience the ups and downs of marriage we know that seeing the couple as a sacrament of God's love to each other, to others, and because of others, obviously doesn't mean "happily ever after," with no problems ever. But it does mean that the love we share has far more at its core than meets the eye, a love and grace like we saw in Greg and his faithful love for Anne and that Julian of Norwich and Brother Lawrence showed us is all around us. With this realization we can begin to appreciate and be aware of all kinds of small "sacraments" in our lives. We can cultivate a sacramental imagination that sees grace in everyday realities. Next, we consider God's call to each couple.

FOR YOUR REFLECTION

(After considering these questions individually I encourage you to talk, as a couple, about some or all of them.)

- One way I can see that our love has been a reflection of grace, of God's love that breaks every expectation, is . . .
- The story of how we met tells a lot about us and about grace because . . .
- Ways that I can now see that I have loved with a limp are . . .
- Some of the ways that I'm aware at times of numbing and avoiding intimacy with you are . . .
- A challenge to forgiveness in our relationship is or was . . .
- I experience you as a tangible sign of God's love when . . .
- One of the ways I can see one of your love languages is when . . .
- Something that is especially sacramental in our marriage is . . .

Listening to Scripture

An invitation to grace from the prophet Isaiah (55:1):

All you who are thirsty, come to the water!

You who have no money, come, buy grain and eat;

Come, buy grain without money, wine and milk

without cost!

FOR FURTHER EXPLORATION

Blaiklock, E.M., Translator. *The Practice of the Presence of God: Based on The Conversations, Letters, Ways and Spiritual Principles of Brother Lawrence, as well as on the writings of Joseph De Beaufort.* Thomas Nelson, 1981. A look at Brother Lawrence's daily awareness of God's grace.

Brown, Brene, *Daring Greatly: How the Courage to Be Vulnerable Transforms the Way We Live, Love, Parent, and Lead.* Avery, 2012. Brown suggests convincingly that vulnerability is the key to growth and personal peace.

Chapman, Gary, *The 5 Love Languages: The Secret to Love That Lasts.* Northfield Publishing, 2015. A helpful invitation to explore the ways we and others experience love.

Finley, Kathleen, *Building a Christian Marriage: Eleven Essential Skills.* Wipf and Stock, 2006. A look at eleven key skills, from learning to love yourself to getting ready to change and grow.

Johnson, Sue, *Hold Me Tight: Seven Conversations for a Lifetime of Love.* Little, Brown, 2008. The developer of Emotionally Focused Therapy shows couples how to be more attached to each other in healthy ways.

Julian of Norwich, *Enfolded in Love: Daily Readings with Julian of Norwich.* Seabury, 1980. Brief excerpts from Julian's writings about God's love and grace.

May, Gerald G., *Addiction and Grace.* Harper & Row, 1988. A look at addiction from a spiritual as well as a psychological perspective.

Powell, John, *Why Am I Afraid to Tell You Who I Am?* Zondervan, 1999. This profound little book shares insights on self-awareness, personal growth and interpersonal communication.

Tutu, Desmond and Mpho Tutu, *The Book of Forgiving: The Fourfold Path for Healing Ourselves and Our World.* HarperOne, 2014. Desmond Tutu and his daughter offer a practical handbook on the process of forgiveness, incorporating the four steps of Telling the Story, Naming the Hurt, Granting Forgiveness and Renewing or Releasing the Relationship.

Chapter Two

Called to Be More
Vocation In Our Marriage

THE WORD VOCATION LITERALLY means a call. Although we will shortly consider the experience of a vocation from God within marriage, we start by considering, instead, two people who lived their vocations within vowed religious life in the twentieth century. As we look we will discover in each of their lives a vocation within a vocation within a vocation.

OUR GUIDES: THOMAS MERTON AND SR. THEA BOWMAN

Thomas Merton is probably the best-known monk of our time. Before his untimely death in 1968 he was also an author who had been outspoken against war and racism and a prophetic voice for peace and nonviolence. He documented his search for his true vocation in his spiritual autobiography, *The Seven Storey Mountain*, a best-seller when it came out in 1949.

Orphaned at a young age and educated at excellent schools, Merton found that the freedom and pleasure of his youth eventually felt hollow and empty until he entered a Trappist monastery. As he grew as a monk and man of prayer, he realized that the world that he thought he had left behind was still there in the monastery, a world he was called to love and challenge, as he did in his many writings.

Merton gradually felt drawn to more contemplation and was later given permission to be a hermit, living alone on the monastery grounds. This solitary life didn't limit, however, his connections with his many friends throughout the world and increasingly, toward the end of his life, in other religious traditions. In fact, his untimely death happened when he was visiting Bangkok, Thailand to address an international conference of Christian monks.

What can we learn about our vocation from Thomas Merton? Besides the fact that as we search for our vocation in life it may find us when we least expect it, as it did Merton, we also see that within a vocation can lie many other unexpected vocations. The young man who entered the monastery had no idea he would end up as a respected author, a voice for peace and nonviolence, and a hermit known around the world.

We also see a vocation within a vocation in the life of Sr. Thea Bowman, an African American woman religious born in rural Mississippi in 1937. After attending a Catholic grade school run by Franciscan sisters she decided to enter their convent at the age of sixteen, the only black face in a white midwestern religious community. She began to realize over time that as a black Catholic woman she had much to bring to the white Euro-American church. She asked herself what it meant to be black and Catholic. It means, she concluded, that she brought to her church herself, her black self, all that she was, all that she had, all that she hoped to become. She brought her whole self, her traditions, her experience, her culture, her African-American songs and dances and gestures and movement and teaching and preaching and healing and responsibility—all as gifts to the church.

Bring it she did, indeed. Sr. Thea helped to found the Institute for Black Catholic Studies at Xavier University in New Orleans and began to speak powerfully before many groups about her own experience. As a layperson she was not allowed to preach in the Catholic Church, but she didn't let that stop her. God, she believed, had called all Christians to speak the word that is Christ, that is truth and salvation. And, she said, if we speak that word in love and faith, with patience and prayer and perseverance, it will take root. For this word has the power to save all.

Late in her life Thea had one more challenge to her vocation: breast cancer. She continued to speak and travel as long as she could, even speaking before the U.S. Catholic bishops. By the time she finished her speech, the bishops were on their feet with Sr. Thea singing "We Shall Overcome!"

At the end of her life, Sister Thea showed the courage, energy and trust in God which had characterized her whole life and vocation, drawing her closer to God by becoming more fully who she was and who God had called her to be.

Now let's see how this experience of vocation—and perhaps several vocations within the main vocation—that we find in Thomas Merton and Thea Bowman may manifest itself in marriage.

GEORGE AND AMY

George still wonders some days. Should he have stayed in the seminary and completed his studies for ordination to the priesthood? When he entered the seminary he was convinced he had a vocation to be a priest and to serve others in that way. But then Amy happened in his life, and things were never quite the same. Her energy and joy helped him to know God's love more deeply in his life, and his spiritual director helped him to see that being with her was where God was calling him. George had understood a vocation as a call from God to serve in the priesthood or religious life, which it certainly can be, but we now understand that God can call us to the vocation of marriage or single life as well.

EXPERIENCING A CALL

What is a vocation, anyway? It is experiencing a call originating from God that attracts us toward a particular way of living out the mission that we all receive: to live out our baptism by being God's love in the world. We are to *be* love. In the mid-1960s, Vatican Council II reminded us that *all of us* are called to holiness, not just the ordained or vowed ones who may look like the "specialists" in the Church. We are to be the body of Christ, his feet and hands, in the world in which we live.

But what does that look like, practically speaking? A vocation to any walk of life doesn't come out of nowhere, of course; it comes from a specific past for each of us. What specific interests and hobbies did I have growing up? What abilities and talents did I have ? How did I interact with friends and family and other people in my life? What questions and fascinations were there for me during those years? These lay the groundwork for my life direction in all kinds of ways.

CAREFUL LISTENING

Listening to a vocation takes reflection and prayer, at least at key points in our lives, or else we'll just be following what others want us to do or what is convenient in our lives. Parker Palmer, in his lovely book *Let Your Life*

Speak, wisely points out that before you tell your life what you plan to do with it, listen for what your life intends to do with you. Before you tell your life what truths and values you plan to live up to, allow your life tell you the truths you embody and the values you stand for.

Much of our lives can be seen in the decisions we make and how we make them; we weave a distinctive pattern of our lives through those decisions, which we'll explore more when we discuss discernment. The key decisions we make, which may often be clear to us only after the fact, can give us important data about our sense of vocation.

Interestingly, another key piece of information about our vocation can come through the choices that *don't work out* the way we would have hoped, even though we've given it our best effort. This can range from past attempts to change our habits to a dating relationship that didn't work out well, even to divorce or the death of a spouse. Each event has something to teach us if we listen to the situation, and it will end up changing us in some way. If we don't learn what we need to from the first experience, then it will probably happen in another variation until we "get" what we need to learn there.

Just as with our sense of love and grace, our sense of vocation happens long before we meet a prospective spouse. All our past experiences impact who each of us is and our particular vocation. For example, we have a good friend who is a priest and also a physician who worked with many low-income mothers through the years as they prepared to give birth. The vocations of both priest and doctor are quite important to this man's overall vocation.

MARRIAGE AS A VOCATION

When I taught a university course on marriage for many years my students often asked how one can know whether a particular person is "the right one." Most couples, when asked that question about their own experience, would say something like, "You just know." I would often tell my students when asked this question that it's more about *being* the right person than about *meeting* the right one.

When we *do* meet the right person, our vocation doesn't stop with being married. I like to think about *marrying* as a process rather than *married* as a static reality. We're engaged in a very long conversation, over a lifetime, which we opt to be involved in. As we begin our marriage, we choose to be changed together—although not identically. Differences in our temperaments may complicate this process. Am I an extrovert or an introvert, someone comfortable with change or not? An idea person or. a practical sort? We'll examine this dynamic between a couple in more detail when we discuss asceticism.

OUR UNIQUE SPIRITUALITY

I have come to believe that each marriage has a unique spirituality, a vocation which takes shape from several sources. Among these are the unique personalities of the spouses and any special gifts and/or interests that each one brings. (Remember, when I use the word "spirituality" here, I mean the the ways I or we live in light of what we believe.) This vocation is who a couple *is*. Others experience that distinctive vocation when they spend time with this couple, but rarely does it register explicitly. I think of it as a unique couple spirituality or couple-personality, the way they are when they're together. The Jesuit theologian and philosopher Pierre Teilhard de Chardin called this union, or relationship of love, a Third Self or a higher soul. This spirituality and couple-vocation can blossom into a family spirituality if children come along.

Over time, our marriage and family life take on a personality of their own with a number of qualities. Some of these are hospitality, traditions, faith, service, education, the arts, work, activities, simplicity, and humor. Each home has some of of these, but they are emphasized to a different degree in different marriages and families. Let's examine each in turn and see how they might take shape in a particular marriage and family. As we do so, keep in mind couples and families you know and how they may live out these qualities.

HOSPITALITY

Herb and Mary Ann Martin love to entertain, and their guests know they will be treated like members of the family when they visit. It doesn't take much of an occasion for the Martins to have what they call a party; in fact, friends know that they are more than welcome in the Martin home if they just drop in.

Many couples and families like Mary Ann and Herb have a special ability to make friends feel welcome and to help strangers feel like friends. They warmly welcome you into their home in ways that seem easy and effortless; they're not worried about how the house looks or how bare the cupboard might be, knowing that having you in their home is the most important part of their lives for now.

In homes like these, kids and teens feel comfortable and not like they're intruding or imposing. Occasionally, there may even be an extra child or adult staying in the home because they need someplace to stay temporarily. This gift of hospitality is often multi-generational, with the younger ones picking up the graciousness from parents or grandparents.

On the other hand, this gift may not be as prominent for a particular couple or family. They may be more introverted so they are not as naturally comfortable with guests. Such couples or families prefer their privacy and keep their social contacts more at a minimum. But they may also be inclined to share other gifts such as financial resources or a talent for inspiring others to cultivate a more authentic faith.

TRADITIONS

Maria and Guillermo Flores are getting ready to celebrate *Dia de Muertos*, the Day of the Dead, to celebrate their deceased relatives, while other families in their neighborhood are making last-minute preparations for Halloween. They had the *quinceañera* celebration for their daughter a couple of months ago, with a special blessing and dress and party for her to mark her passage into adulthood at fifteen and to thank God for who she is and who she's becoming. When St. Patrick's Day rolls around, the Murphys down the street will celebrate their Irish heritage again this year, complete with corned beef and cabbage and even some green beer.

Couples and families like the Flores and Murphy families that have a strong sense of tradition and celebrations can be fun to be around. There is often something to celebrate, whether birthdays or religious or ethnic holidays. They adopt practices from their ethnic backgrounds, in their own unique ways. They have a strong sense of "This-is-how-we-do-it-here" which may also include special wedding and funeral traditions.

These traditions and rituals, for the Flores and the Murphys and others like them, help remind them of who they are. It gives the extended family something to count on, year after year. But that doesn't mean that these celebrations can't be added to or changed, as the times and individuals change.

In other families where this quality is not as strong, there isn't a strong continuity between one year and the next, and there may be years when certain occasions are not celebrated at all, and that's okay with the family members.

FAITH AND RELIGION

Joe and Maureen Collins and their three children are active in their parish in various ways, but their faith goes beyond what happens in their parish. Besides meal and bedtime prayers together each night, they gather to reflect on the Sunday readings and also pray the Rosary together toward the end of the week.

For couples and families like the Collinses, faith and religious practice is a shared reality, perhaps reflected in religious art in the home or religious books or music present there. Religion is more than just an individual reality, and it shows itself in more than regular church-going. Faith is an explicit part of how they do what they do, and as a family they pray regularly for people they know who have asked for their prayer support.

In other homes where this is not as strong a quality there is still a strong spirituality, but it may not be as explicit as *shared* faith activities. If faith and religious observance happen in such marriages or families, it's more at the individual level. This may be the case, for example, in interfaith marriages, but there can also be a strong shared understanding in such homes.

SERVICE

For Katie and Ben Prentice volunteering and service have always been a way of life; in fact, it was the way they met when they both were serving in the Peace Corps. As their children grow, Ben and Katie often bring them along to places where they volunteer, like providing hospitality for homeless families once a month at their parish.

Couples and families like the Prentices know that "love thy neighbor" is not just theoretical. They can be seen regularly involved in service projects at school, soup kitchens, food banks or other nonprofits. These experiences help their world to be broader than it is for many other families, whether through contact with refugees or with families in other parts of our ever-smaller globe. This vocation may also take the shape of involvement in local or regional politics to try to make conditions better for others. These couples and families know that when they help others they benefit at least as much as those they help.

In families where service is not as explicit an activity serving others still happens. For example, in shared chores at home. The focus may not extend beyond the walls of their own home except through donations to nonprofit organizations. But the service remains just as authentic.

EDUCATION

For as long as they can remember, learning has been important for Dan and Sue Nguyen. Not only did their parents insist on good grades when they were growing up, but their parents also modeled the importance of schooling, continuing to ask questions and finding out new information as they aged. Sue and Dan still find that education is key as they keep up in their fields, explore new areas of information, and encourage their kids in school.

Learning starts early and intentionally in homes like the Nguyens where education is a key part of their vocation and spirituality, and it may even take the shape of home schooling. There is exposure to all kinds of questioning, and their contact with various kinds of enrichment, from libraries to the theater, is encouraged. Higher education is also respected and encouraged in such families and couples, and they may limit and monitor the exposure to social media in their lives to strive for a healthy "diet" of information.

By contrast, there are families that don't encourage curiosity and inquiry for its own sake, although they still support going to school. These households may see schooling more as a means of getting a better job instead of as an end in itself.

THE ARTS

Yet another kind of vocation is evident in families like that of Yvonne and Zach Jablonsky, where music, dance, art, sculpture and other creative pursuits are encouraged. Yvonne almost pursued dance professionally, but ended up deciding on a different career path. One of their daughters takes dance, and a son and daughter each play musical instruments.

Both Zach and Yvonne appreciate beauty in many forms, and they encourage lessons, attendance at performances, and an appreciation for artistic accomplishments. Art and beauty are clearly evident in their home. Zach enjoys working with wood, and Yvonne is learning to weave. Working with one's hands, whether in fabric or yarn, wood, clay or other media is often a part of this kind of spirituality.

In other homes these artistic explorations may not happen as readily because of a lack of support or exposure to the arts. Artistic and musical endeavors may be seen as impractical, something to be pursued only as a hobby, as long as it doesn't distract from more practical pursuits.

WORK

Ellen and Steve Cook have always worked hard, ever since they were able to do so. Steve's family worked in banking for a couple of generations, but he found that he enjoyed helping people in direct sales instead. For many years, Ellen helped maintain the office for a dentist, and her boss says that he doesn't know what he would do without her.

For most of us our work—and not just our paid employment—is an important part of our individual vocations as well as that of a couple or family. Work can shape us, and we shape it as well. Our vocation can have as much to do with *how* we do our work as much as *what* we do.

In some homes work is more important than it is in others. That may have to do with a particular kind of career or work, perhaps with a family business or a particular profession that holds an attraction for several family members, such as teaching or medicine. The ability to balance work and home is never easy, especially when an increasing number of women work outside the home and are not focused only on what happens in the home. On the other hand, times of unemployment can be a tremendous challenge for a family.

Success may be quite important in these homes, perhaps extending to pressure on younger generations to exceed the financial and professional accomplishments of their elders. In some families competition is a way to encourage this excellence, and it may take the form of games in the family, whether board or electronic, complete with some family members who feel that they must always strive to win.

In other homes success at employment or career or games is not as big a focus, as long as whatever a family member is involved in makes that person happy.

Competition may also extend in some families to sports and outdoor activities, including individual or team activities throughout the year. The Wilsons are a good example of this because they have their favorite teams and love to cheer them on, but for them it's not just a couch-potato interest in sports. From school days on, Tom Wilson and his siblings have had a focus on fitness and sportsmanship, and when he was growing up each family member was expected to find an activity or two that kept him or her active, often including a friendly pick-up basketball game around the holidays.

Outdoors activities are often important, too. Whether it's going to a favorite cabin or campground, lake, river or ocean beach, being in nature renews their spirituality. When the weather starts to warm up, they can't wait to get outdoors.

Other families are not as focused on sports and fitness and the outdoors, at least as a family, although those activities may be a value for some individuals. Staying fit and physically active is not as big a shared goal for some.

SIMPLICITY

When Karen and Jim O'Connor were starting their life together, they didn't have much. Their possessions were minimal, most of them secondhand or used and mismatched. As their lives became more established, they made a decision not to accumulate more possessions and furniture than they really needed because they appreciated the freedom that came with having fewer possessions. As a result, their home is simpler than other couples they know, whose lives are more affluent than theirs.

Some couples, like Jim and Karen, continue to keep their lives as simple and uncluttered as possible, knowing that they're "swimming upstream" in a culture that tells them that they should get a new sofa or recliner or bedroom set or even just a new gadget. For some of these couples mobility in jobs or being in the military may contribute to the need for a minimum of possessions.

On the other hand, some families seek a more comfortable lifestyle, which may include collecting antiques, heirlooms, or other "nice things." Many of these things come with a story from past generations, giving the family a special sense of home.

HUMOR

In families like that of Grace and Tim Whelan, where humor is a big part of their spirituality, you never know when the joke may be on you. You'll frequently hear laughter in their house, often for no apparent reason, and someone may want to tell you the latest joke they heard. These families are often able to laugh at themselves and be silly at times, but you may want to watch out for the odd pun or the practical joke when you're there.

Many times humor happens in the context of stories and storytelling, especially the stories about Tim's old pickup and the adventures he's had with it, which helps everyone appreciate the goodness as well as the fallibility of family members. They're careful to make sure that the humor is not at someone else's expense or sarcastic in tone. At the Whelans' house there are serious times when the occasion calls for it, but more often than not life is approached with a light touch and a giggle.

In other families the focus may be more on what is serious and impor-tant in life, while laughter and silliness take a back seat .

❖ ❖ ❖

These are only some of the variables which can take shape in the unique vocation of each couple and family, in their living out of the universal call to holiness in very different ways in different contexts and situations. This one-of-a-kind vocation takes time to unfold, but over months and years it becomes clear that each couple and family is indeed a unique story of love that God tells with our help. It's important to recall that any of these variables—hospitality, traditions, faith and religion, service, education, the arts, work, activities, simplicity, and humor—can be out of balance and can disrupt the vocation and spirituality of the couple or family if they become an end in themselves. Balance is the hallmark of a healthy vocation and spirituality.

❖ ❖ ❖

George, whom we met at the beginning of this chapter, can see more and more that he and Amy have been building a strong vocation and spirituality, one just as holy as the spirituality of those who are called to priesthood and religious life, and one that helps express the myriad ways we can live in the light of God's love in our lives. Just like Thomas Merton and Thea Bowman, the vocation that God has in mind for a couple may continue to surprise us as we live it out. Next we explore how others are involved in our vocation.

FOR YOUR REFLECTION:

(After considering these individually I encourage you to talk, as a couple, about some or all of them.)

- When I think about my growing up years, one early trait of mine that stands out is. . .

- An example of a decision that didn't work out the way I hoped and that helped me grow is . . .

- How have our past experiences, together and apart, contributed to who we were when we met and who we are now?

- When I think of how my life would have been different without you, I . . .

- When and how did we know we were the "right one" for each other?

- How have we seen our "very long conversation with each other" change and deepen through the years? If you had told me when we married that we would end up . . . I would not have believed you.

- What are some of the qualities that we would use to describe the unique vocation of our marriage? Would they include hospitality, traditions, faith, service, education, the arts, work, activities, simplicity or humor? Are any of these out of balance for us?

Listening to Scripture

Our vocation from God in the prophet Isaiah (43:1):

But now, thus says the Lord, who created you, Jacob,
and formed you, Israel:
Do not fear, for I have redeemed you; I have called you
by name: you are mine.

FOR FURTHER EXPLORATION

Cole, Casey, OFM, *Called: What Happens After Saying Yes to God*. Franciscan Media, 2018. While he was in formation as a Franciscan, the author reflected on his vocation and the vocation of all Christians.

Merton, Thomas, *The Seven Storey Mountain:* Harcourt, Brace, 1947. Thomas Merton's autobiographical account of his experience of the call to become Catholic and to enter the monastic life.

Oliva, Max, S.J., *Beatitudes for the Workplace*. Novalis, 2009. Fr. Max discusses how the virtues of wisdom, integrity, honesty, compassion, justice for the earth, forgiveness, generosity and courage can shape how we approach work and our decisions.

Palmer, Parker, *Let Your Life Speak: Listening for the Voice of Vocation*. Jossey-Bass, 2000. Palmer draws on his Quaker background to help the reader see the gift that is one's vocation in life.

Pierce, Gregory F. A., *Spirituality at Work: 10 Ways to Balance Your Life on the Job*. Loyola, 2005. Since work is such a big part of our lives and our vocation, Pierce gives practical suggestions on how to enhance our awareness of our spirituality on the job.

Smith, Charlene and John Feister, *Thea's Song: The Life of Thea Bowman*. Orbis, 2012. A thorough and inspiring look at Sr. Thea Bowman and her life.

Chapter Three

We Are Not Alone

Community In Our Marriage

BEFORE WE CONSIDER THE ways in which others impact us in our lives and our marriages—even when we least expect it and can't seem to see it or feel it—we will consider two amazing women, one contemporary and one who lived more than a century ago. Both of these women help expand our ideas about who might be included in our sense of community, who is a part of "us" and we of them, beyond the people we might usually think of or with whom we are more comfortable. This awareness is especially impressive in light of the larger North American culture of individualism in which they both have lived.

OUR GUIDES: DOROTHY DAY AND HARRIET TUBMAN

Dorothy Day was quite unlikely in many ways to have had the impact she did have on the Church, especially to have been considered in 1980 at her death the most influential, interesting and significant figure in the history of American Catholicism. She had no real religious formation when she was growing up during the early part of the twentieth century and spent her college years surrounded by radicals who were involved in the popular protests of the day and who saw little use for formal religion.

Her life changed dramatically in 1926 with the birth of her daughter, Tamar, whom she chose to raise as a Catholic. Near the same time, Dorothy chose to convert to Catholicism herself. This led to the end of Dorothy's relationship with the baby's father, the love of Dorothy's life and a man who didn't believe in marriage or religion. A few years later, in 1932, she met Peter Maurin, an itinerant philosopher and agitator, who helped her see the connections between her new faith and a radical concern for the rights and dignity of others, which had always been her focus.

She remembered reading as a child about the saints and how their sacrifices in giving their lives for the sick, the maimed, and the leper had thrilled her. But she also remembered wondering why all their energy was spent in remedying the evil instead of avoiding it in the first place. Where were the saints trying to change the social order, to do away with slavery, for example, not just minister to the slaves?

Together Dorothy and Peter Maurin founded the Catholic Worker movement, which helped expand people's horizons when it came to those they cared about, including the poor, the unemployed and underemployed at the time of the Great Depression. This eventually included even the enemy in their pacifist positions during World War II and in conflicts since then. Dorothy Day did this through the Catholic Worker newspaper, distributed on the streets of New York and elsewhere and still available today, still only a penny a copy. She and others also began houses of hospitality, places where the poor, hungry and homeless could find a meal and perhaps a place to stay. Although each house is independent, there are still about 250 Catholic Worker houses around the world, over 200 of which are in the U.S.

Dorothy gave us a powerful example of how to connect her radical care for and passion about all others and her deep and traditional Catholic faith. She took the works of mercy literally: "I was hungry and you gave me to eat . . ." but she also saw her role as a Christian to help work for systemic political change and encourage critical reflection on social issues in light of faith.

Harriet Tubman was born into slavery about a century earlier than Dorothy, and the date of her birth is approximate because from the very beginnings of her life she experienced the harsh realities of slave life, including frequent beatings and indignities. But something in her knew that she was meant for freedom, and that conviction was tied deeply to her faith in God and to her early visionary experiences of being called to the freedom to which Moses had led his people in the Bible. Harriet was small and wiry and used to hard work and being outdoors; that and her ability to move quietly and confidently in the dark helped her when she headed to freedom, following the North Star through swamps and forests, sleeping and hiding out by day.

When she arrived safely in Pennsylvania she couldn't believe how different the world seemed to her now that she was free. But she quickly realized that there was more that God was calling her to than just her own freedom; she had crossed the line and now was free, but those she had left behind in slavery should also be free. With God's help she would lead them north to freedom also.

In an extremely dangerous environment she decided to help others and did an amazing job of it: over the next twelve years she returned nineteen times to the South and rescued at least three hundred slaves, including her own parents. Leading twenty or thirty people at a time, some of them children, to freedom was far trickier than traveling by herself, but she never lost one of her charges, even after the 1850 Fugitive Slave Act meant that she had to take them farther north to Canada to be safe. She was eventually helped by a network of safe houses and helpers, the famous Underground Railroad. Even in her helping others she had help from yet another community of support.

Harriet was hated by the bounty hunters and whites in the South, who put a high price on her head, but she was called "Moses" by her own people. During the Civil War years she helped the Union Army as a nurse, a scout and even a spy. She later retired but continued to help poor blacks and to support herself by selling vegetables that she raised. She lived into her nineties, rarely recognized for all the ways in which she continued to dedicate herself to a freedom that was not just for herself alone while others in her community weren't yet free.

Both Harriet Tubman and Dorothy Day not only help us see how connected we are to one another, but they also expand our vision of what that sense of the other might include. They did this not just by talking about how to live more inclusively but by actually doing so themselves. They gathered others together, whether today or in the days of slavery, to help carry out this mission in the midst of our busy, individualistic world. Let us, with that in mind, explore how the element of community impacts our marriages.

NANCY AND BOB

Whenever Nancy begins to think that she's alone in her marriage, far away from her family and some of her oldest friends, she remembers her wedding day and the awesome experience of looking out on so many people in her and Bob's lives who had helped them to be who they were as they now prepared to promise the rest of their lives to each other. Yes, there were a few cousins who couldn't make it and a few people who knew their parents better than they knew Bob and Nancy, but overall the people there had given themselves and their yeses to Bob or Nancy or both of them throughout their lives and now had made it possible for the two of them to say yes to each other.

At our own wedding many years ago now, Father Tom, a long-time family friend, reminded us, "There are many people who have been God's love for the two of you in your lives; now you are to be the main shape of that love for each other." Just as our friendships are a key part of who we each are individually, those who surround us as a couple give us new energy, and we can also give life to them.

EASY TO OVERLOOK COMMUNITY

It's easy for us to forget that we live in what may be the most individualistic society the world has ever known, a culture that thinks we can each make it on our own. This view goes all the way back to the Enlightenment (17th and 18th centuries) and the idea that "I think therefore I am." (René Descartes) That is in strong contrast to cultural concepts such as the African term *ubuntu.* This is a Bantu word that implies "I am because we are." I am a person because, and only because, of my relationships.

In a private and individualistic culture we can still remember that we are not people of faith on our own; after all, we say "*Our* Father," not "*My* Father." We talk about being members of the body of Christ and the communion of saints. It is easy for us to lose sight of the fact that we are surrounded by those who care about us and help us to believe. We are each a *web of relationships.* Notice how in conversations it doesn't take long before the significant people in our lives pop up in a reference or thought of some kind. In fact, one way to think about *remembering* is to see that this word means "to *recall again* that we are *members* of one another."

Although it might seem that the technology around us these days helps keep us in touch with others, the intimacy that it encourages can be a poor substitute for the real thing. Sue Johnson, the founder of Emotionally Focused Therapy, reminds us in her book *Love Sense: The Revolutionary New Science of Romantic Relationships,* that we become accustomed to the simplified, the superficial, and the sensational in our lives. Whether it's pornography or stories of celebrities, we settle for something artificial rather than learning to craft our own relationships.

Mobility is another factor that works against our connection with others. When most of us think back to our wedding, like Nancy we are aware that many of the people with whom we were close at that time, we are not physically or emotionally close to now, and others have taken their place. Our lives shift, and many of us have relocated, perhaps several times in the course of the years. But we are still more connected to that ever-shifting web of relationships than we know.

OUR FAMILY BACKGROUNDS

As I have worked with engaged couples through the years I became more and more convinced of how important our family systems are to who we are as we marry. We'd like to think that we're not that heavily influenced by our family of origin, but encountering others from different backgrounds helps us see how those influences may be more powerful than we thought.

The film "My Big Fat Greek Wedding" is a great example. The main character, Toula, from a strong, boisterous Greek family, has a hard time connecting with her boyfriend, and later fiancé, Ian, who is from quieter and more restrained WASP roots. One of the first places these differences in our families show themselves is when it comes to the holidays; each may have traditions that vary considerably from the other.

So many family variables can come into play for each of us, most of which we're not aware of: from birth order to gender to the way we communicate. Other variables may be more subtle but are nonetheless important, including our expectations of marriage, addictions and illnesses—both physical and mental—our ethnic backgrounds and our closeness to extended family. We are indeed marrying each other's family patchwork.

Some couples, however, don't start out with much of a community. Perhaps there's some opposition to their marriage or they just don't choose to connect with others as much, but eventually they will need to build some kind of a community of support for themselves in order to be able to thrive as a couple.

Other couples have the opposite problem: *too much* community. When there's a conflict with one or both families that they can't seem to handle effectively, they may have to put distance—physical or emotional or both—between them and others. Working on those boundaries is almost never easy, but it can be so important. I often recommend Henry Cloud and John Townsend's book, *Boundaries: When to Say Yes, How to Say No To Take Control of Your Life.*

Because our families, of any size, are systems and any system tends to resist change, then any shift, whether marrying or relocating or starting or adding to the family, is going to meet resistance. Even when it's a good and exciting change, it can still cause anxiety. The film "Father of the Bride" takes this dynamic to a humorous extreme. This business of being connected to others can get messy indeed at times.

A KIND OF TRINITY

As we become a couple, even before the wedding, we are invited to become a "community" of love for each other, a kind of Trinity. In that sense, this love surrounding the two of us, a love that was clearly part of each of us, also has its own identity, its own "personality:" an "us-ness." So, between us there is you, me and *us*: a certain "community" from the beginning.

As we continue to experience the grace between us that comes, of course, from God's grace, our goal then becomes trying to approach the complete giving and sharing, the delighting in one another that we can only begin to imagine in the Holy Trinity. Most of the time what we have with each other is certainly far from that mutuality, but every once in a while, with a shared project or teamwork, we can glimpse something of that "Trinitarian" energy.

OUR COMMUNITY GROWS

If children come along, the energy in this community of ours quickly begins to change, even with the pregnancy or the too-long process of waiting for an adoptive child. Many questions begin to bubble up with each child, not just with the first: Who will this child be? Will we be able to love this child enough? How will this event stretch our community and our ability to love?

The reality is that we will never be the same again; "we" are now far more complex than we were before. And yet what we are growing to be is rooted in the "us" we've already established, and it will continue to be nourished from that source. Our new "us" is taking shape now, and before we know it, our "us" will be walking around, part of us and yet not us, someone new in the world, which we'll explore further when we examine incarnation.

HOW DOES COMMUNITY HAPPEN?

After we're married and on our own, how do we begin to build a community of support, to be intentional about its presence in our lives? It can be tricky for young couples to find other couples with whom both spouses are comfortable. Neighbors and coworkers are natural sources, and at times our lives and needs can end up shaping this dynamic in our lives. The families of our kids' friends and our neighbors can also easily end up being friends for life.

It may helpful to be intentional about connections for each one of us at times, from finding a men's or women's group, or perhaps a book group or one focused around a hobby like sewing or cars or music, especially as the kids are leaving home, if there are children. Whether for one or both of us, we need the connections with others which help us to thrive. What is important here is that as a couple we are able to have good "soil" for the "plant" of our marriage, surrounding ourselves with people who have similar values and who can encourage us as often as we encourage them.

Ironically, one way we know the importance of this strong community of couples and families is when it comes apart. When we hear, for example, of a couple we have known splitting up and planning on getting a divorce, it can hit like a blow to the solar plexus, leaving us wondering what went wrong and how else we might have been able to help support them.

A BROADER COMMUNITY

Some families and couples naturally widen their sense of community far beyond the nuclear and even the extended family. Some extend hospitality to foreign students or visitors, or have a number of contacts and friends because of overseas travel or from living overseas. Yet another way that the boundaries are extended may have to do with having an international or intercultural marriage, one where differences in food, clothes, customs, and expectations are regularly challenged or expanded.

SOLITUDE—ALONE AND TOGETHER

As much as others are important, perhaps essential, to who we are as a couple and as individuals, we also need to spend thoughtful time alone, individually and as a couple.

The time of solitude for each of us individually helps us recover and renew who we each are and to reflect on what's happening currently in our lives. Although introverts may need more of this time to do the inner processing that happens before they're ready to interact with others, the extroverts among us need solitude, too. There's a lovely You Tube reflection, "How To Be Alone," that explores this well and shows how solitude is quite different from loneliness.

The time of solitude that each spouse takes can actually help the marriage because we can appreciate each other more when we're apart and have more to share with each other when we come back together later. It's important to be aware of and honor the fact that each of us has a different need and pacing for our times of solitude.

Just as we each need time alone away from each other, we also need time alone as a couple to nourish our relationship, away from family and friends, and even children. A date night once a week for lo, these many years, has been an invaluable way for my husband and me to reaffirm our connection and importance as a couple, even in the face of strong challenges. It is a practice that we still continue, long after our children have left home.

❖ ❖ ❖

The more Nancy contemplates the people that have been part of her and Bob's lives, the more she can see that those who were there to support them at their wedding and before were just part of the picture of all those who have helped the two of them to keep saying yes to each other through the years. And that community of support has continued to grow and expand through the years, like the ways that both Dorothy Day and Harriet Tubman challenged people to expand their circle of caring and love. Let's see next how we each need to set aside our own needs for the good of us as a couple at times.

FOR YOUR REFLECTION:

After considering these questions individually I encourage you to talk about some or all of them as a couple:

- One way our family background affects us that I didn't expect is . . .

- One of the biggest challenges that we have had from our families is . . .

- I witnessed our extended family resist change when . . .

- One effect technology has on our relationship is . . .

- Two ways our community of support has changed since our marriage is . . .

- I don't know if we could have made it through the challenge of . . . without the support of our friends and family.

- Two ways children changed our spirituality are . . .

- We have done a . . . job when it comes to individual time for solitude and date nights for us as a couple.

> ## Listening to Scripture
>
> *Our call to community from John's Gospel (13:34–35):*
> I give you a new commandment: love one another.
> As I have loved you, so you also should love one
> another. This is how all will know that you are my
> disciples, if you have love for one another."

FOR FURTHER EXPLORATION

Battle, Michael. *Ubuntu: I in You and You in Me.* Seabury, 2009. A clear, helpful introduction to the idea of Ubuntu and its implications for a Western understanding.

Clinton, Catherine. *Harriet Tubman: The Road to Freedom.* Little, Brown, 2005. The definitive biography of one of the most courageous women in American history.

Cloud, Henry and Townsend, John. *Boundaries: When to Say Yes, How to Say No to Take Control of Your Life.* Zondervan, 1992. A classic with a faith perspective on how to be clear with others so that one is not taken advantage of.

Forest, Jim. *Love is the Measure: A Biography of Dorothy Day.* Orbis, 1993. A good introduction to the life of Dorothy Day, founder of the Catholic Worker.

Johnson, Sue. *Love Sense: The Revolutionary New Science of Romantic Relationships.* Little Brown, 2013. Based on the science of emotional bonding, this resource shows us how we are built to need each other and how to enhance that.

Lanier, Sarah A. *Foreign to Familiar: A Guide to Understanding Hot—and Cold-Climate Cultures.* McDougal Publishing, 2000. A fascinating look at how culture and climate affect many variables, including individualism vs. group orientation and inclusion vs. privacy.

Rohlheiser, Ronald, *The Holy Longing: The Search for a Christian Spirituality.* Doubleday, 1999. Fr. Rohlheiser clearly explores how we need one another in the church, as well as a number of other important topics.

Chapter Four

Setting Aside the Self
Asceticism in Our Marriage

ASCETICISM—SETTING ASIDE MY OWN needs and preferences for a higher purpose—may seem miles away from what happens in a marriage. But before we examine that more closely, let's make sure that we have a clear idea of what asceticism can look like, first in a dramatic fashion and then in a more everyday way. We'll see two figures from the late 19th century who are both quite different from each other in how they lived out their asceticism and also quite similar in the strength of their ability to set aside their own wants for those of others.

OUR GUIDES: DAMIEN OF MOLOKAI
AND THÉRÈSE OF LISIEUX

Fr. Damien de Veuster, born in Belgium in 1840, had become a priest of the Sacred Heart Fathers and was grateful to have been sent to Hawaii as a missionary, since being in the missions had always been his goal. After serving in the islands for nine years, in 1873 he requested a high-risk assignment indeed: serving the lepers in the isolated colony on the island of Molokai.

When Westerners "discovered" the Hawaiian Islands in the late 18th century they brought with them a number of diseases to which the native population had no immunity, including Hansen's Disease (leprosy), which reached epidemic proportions in Hawaii within 40 years and for centuries defied cure or remedy around the world. The only approach that had been used to that point was to isolate those infected so that the disease didn't spread to others through close contact.

By the time Damien arrived on Molokai he found a community without hope, since those exiled to the island were under a virtual death sentence and literally dumped there, even having to swim to shore from a boat. Once they got to the grim village on the island, they found a place without dignity for those living there, even in death. There was a lack of decent homes for those suffering from leprosy, but within several years Fr. Damien helped change a great deal about their standard of living and their activities, as well as their physical and spiritual care. At the same time, he continued to preach against the drinking and immorality practiced by those who felt they were already condemned to die.

Damien didn't shrink from close contact with those to whom he ministered and included himself among the inhabitants of the island. He explained in a letter to his brother in Europe that in preaching he always included himself among their number, saying "we lepers," not "my brethren" to help bring everyone to Christ. Eventually, Damien's manner of speaking became literally the truth as the disease began to claim his body, too, a result of how closely he lived with the people.

Damien continued to work tirelessly for his people, even though now he had to share their isolation and the devastation of the disease. He couldn't even meet privately for the sacrament of Confession. Instead, he had to yell from one boat to another when the bishop came close to shore. He died among the lepers on the island, forbidden to visit his mission headquarters in Honolulu for fear of contagion. Damien gave his life and all he had for people whom most of the world shunned and forgot. His asceticism, more extreme than most of us can imagine, had been life-changing for the mission where he served.

Although St. Thérèse of Lisieux had also wanted to be a missionary, she ended up practicing asceticism in a quiet and hidden way. Born to a middle-class family in France in the late 19th century, Thérèse was was the youngest of five girls whose mother died when her youngest daughter was only four. She and her father were close, but at the young age of 15, by special permission, Thérèse was allowed to enter a cloistered Carmelite convent where two of her older sisters were already members of the community, and other members of the family would later join them. Remaining there until her early death, the future saint's life as a nun was filled with spiritual growth and a powerful example of a unique approach to asceticism.

She had always been strong-willed, even spoiled, and in the convent she set her determined mind to the goal of being a saint. Thérèse pursued this goal through what she called her "Little Way." This meant performing her everyday actions faithfully and suffering each petty insult or injury in the presence of, and for the love of, God. It's easy for people who have never lived in religious life, especially in a contemplative order, to assume that it's an easy and rather stress-free environment. That's not what Thérèse found there, however. Rather, it was a serious challenge to live with a nun who made irritating noises with her mouth behind Thérèse in chapel. Likewise, living with an older sister whom she was assigned to help but who never seemed to be grateful for or satisfied with her help was a significant challenge. Thérèse discovered many opportunities to disregard her natural inclination to throw a tantrum and get her own way.

We know about Thérèse's spiritual struggles from the publication, after her death, of her autobiography, *The Story of a Soul*. She was ordered to write it by the prioress who was, in fact, her older sister Pauline. Thérèse saw herself as of little account, a "little flower." Yet there was nothing romantic or sentimental about her use of this image. Rather, it was a way to convey the idea of strength in weakness, much as St. Paul did in 2 Corinthians 12:10: "I am content with weaknesses, insults, hardships, persecutions, and difficulties for Christ's sake. For when I am weak, then I am strong." Thérèse had in mind the delicate flower that takes root and thrives in a crack in a rock or in dry, rocky ground, and there is nothing romantic or sentimental about this.

Thérèse knew she was precious in the eyes of God and could do little things with great love for God. This brings to mind the way in which Thérèse was asked to give herself completely to God. In the last years of her life she suffered from tuberculosis, and she endured a great deal of pain. She showed many people that each moment, accepted and lived in a spirit of love, is a way to draw closer to God by offering our "little things," our everyday irritations and daily chores, to God. She died in 1897 at the age of only 24 and, remarkably, was declared a saint in 1925.

With the powerful examples of Damien of Molokai and Thérèse of Lisieux let's look at asceticism as the setting aside of what I might want for a greater good, namely love of God and love of others. Let's examine how this might take shape in marriage.

GEORGE AND SARAH

George was tired of hearing tiny Zachary cry at night and weary from having to get up to bring the baby to his wife Sarah so that she could nurse him back to sleep. After all, George was the one who had to go to work in the morning these days, since Sarah was still on maternity leave from her job.

But, he also realized, when he went off to the office, her "work" was just beginning: that of caring for Zach and his two siblings, none of them old enough to be in school. He gave a sigh and hoisted himself out of bed to go see how the little guy was, check his diaper and bring him back to Mom.

George's tiredness—more than just physical—and his willingness to push beyond it is actually part of the ancient spiritual discipline of asceticism. The word "asceticism" sounds rather grim and has echoes of religious self-denial, austerity and harsh discipline, either imposed or chosen. It can also seem miles away from the everyday life of marriage, but there is a strong connection.

WHAT IS ASCETICISM?

Although asceticism has come to be associated with religious training, it has its roots in the Greek word for athletic training, which is a helpful image here. If I'm trying out for a certain sport, that means I will need to make time for practice and make choices about how much sleep I get. I may even need to make difficult choices about my diet.

I don't choose disciplines for their own sake, but I choose to curtail some of my freedom for the sake of a bigger, better goal. This helps shed some light on the idea of asceticism in marriage. Whether it's George getting up with the baby in the middle of the night or a wife who is willing to do what her husband wants to do for the evening rather than what she'd rather do, asceticism is a daily reality in marriage. As couples we make daily choices that need to take into account the other person and the priority of that relationship in our lives, even though we may never have thought about those choices as asceticism.

BEGINNING AT THE WEDDING

In a Greek or Russian Orthodox wedding, there's a powerful way this call to asceticism is ritualized. At one point in the ceremony the bride and groom both receive beautiful crowns, sometimes linked by a ribbon between them, crowns they will keep and may display later at home. Although the couple may seem to be king and queen for a day at the wedding and later in their new home, a key part of the reason for the crowns is that they are martyrs' crowns. Since a martyr is someone who dies for his or her faith, what does that have to do with marriage?

The orthodox wedding liturgy reminds the couple that often each of them is called in marriage to set aside his or her own will and preferences for the sake of the spouse. This dying to one's self a little each day, a daily kind of martyrdom, is important for the sake of their future life as a couple.

IT'S THE LITTLE THINGS

A marriage may need to deal with a difficult issue, such as a spouse's or child's serious illness or disability, and that builds in a special degree of asceticism. Most don't face these major challenges all that often, but neither is it unusual for this to occur.

An old song says, "Little things mean a lot," especially when it comes to small romantic gestures, but the same is true of the ways this "martyrdom" happens in any marriage, starting with our personal quirks and their challenges. As a couple we appreciate the gift of the other person always being there, *and* we can also gradually see what an *irritant* it is that the other person is *always* there.

One spouse may like to be early to an arranged appointment, while the other is more relaxed about being on time. Or one of us is far neater than the other or likes to plan and have advance notice of what we're doing, while the other likes to be spontaneous. Whatever the differences and tensions between us, these inclinations in the spouse probably aren't going to change. Still, some days these habits and preferences are harder to live with than other days.

Usually one of us is more extroverted and social than the other, which can also present challenges. While an extrovert, who processes his or her thoughts out loud, often wants to talk issues out, an introvert may need more quiet time to process what's happening around him or her and isn't necessarily ready to talk about a problem when asked, "What's wrong?" Also, the quieter person is often more depleted than recharged by being around others and may be ready to go home from a gathering far earlier than the more social spouse, who may just be getting started.

The list of these differences and possible irritants can go on and on and might include levels of cleanliness, preferences for sports and other activities, a choice of pets, where we'd like to live—in the city or the country or close to or far from extended family—and being a morning or a night person.

Each of these is small by itself, but together they add up to significant differences that we need to cope with. No wonder the songwriter Leonard Cohen once remarked:

> I think marriage is the hottest furnace of the spirit today. Much more difficult than solitude, much more challenging for people who want to work on themselves. It's a situation in which there

are no alibis, excruciating most of the time . . . but it's only in this
situation that any kind of work can be done.

The temptation can be strong to ignore these little irritants in the other
person and just live with them. Instead, we are called to the asceticism of
bringing up the uncomfortable issues and talking about our frustrations
instead of letting them fester. Paul Simon, in his song "You're Kind," reminds us of the consequences if we try to ignore the need to face these little
irritants. As he sang: "I like to sleep with the window open, / And you keep
the window closed, / So good-bye, good-bye, good-bye."

LOVE VS. LAW

Thankfully, our faith helps us here. Not only is the spouse the closest "neighbor" I am called to love, but sometimes he or she can feel like the "enemy"
whom I'm also called to love. Jesus can help one to not insist on his or her
preference at all costs, as our culture may encourage. But rather, like Jesus
in agony in the garden as his death approached, we can say with him to God
his Father, " Not my will but yours be done."

In a wise article, "How to Get More Married Each Day," (*US Catholic*,
June 1979) Mary Carson wrote about love versus law. Love she said, is giving freely, expecting nothing in return, while law always wants things fair,
this for that. She wrote that both attitudes are there in any marriage; we still
retain a need to have things work out "fairly." It's as if we carry residuals
from our grade school years and didn't like it when someone else seemed
to get a bigger piece of whatever was being served. We still "keep score" too
often, even in our marriages.

How does this tension between love and law work in practice? Mary
Carson's example helps us here, but it could be about nearly anything.

Suppose a husband is delayed coming home from work. What happens? As far as his wife is concerned, by law she's annoyed that she must
keep dinner waiting. With love, she's concerned that he's had to work late.
By law, she wonders if he's really working or out having a good time while
she's stuck home taking care of the kids and the dead dinner. With love,
she's afraid that he's had an accident and that's why he hasn't called. By law,
if he'd had an accident the police would have called. With love, she knows
he's doing the best he can.

How does the husband react? By law, he knows he's not a child; he
shouldn't have to account for every minute. With love, he doesn't want her
to worry. By law, he knows he's trying to finish a job at the office. He doesn't
know how long he's going to be, so what's he going to tell her if he does call?

With love, he calls and makes a date with her. "Why don't you feed the kids and get them to bed, and maybe we can have supper alone when I get home." By law, why should he bother calling; she's already angry anyway.

If we go back and look at just the responses of love, we can see how much smoother the experience for both spouses could be. When the focus is not on "What about me?" each is worried for the other and less concerned about him- or herself. Mary Carson says that most of us fluctuate back and forth. While we try to aim for the more generous response of love, too often we fall short and end up in the area of law instead, especially in an era of more dual-career and egalitarian couples. ("I emptied the dishwasher twice this week; it's your turn.")

A QUESTION OF BALANCE

Does this mean that we *always* need to be patient and giving in the face of irritating behaviors from our spouse and even disregard disrespectful or unhealthy comments or actions? Where is the line that can help us see when frustrating and difficult behavior crosses over into putdowns and emotional or verbal abuse, which should never be allowed?

This line can be much harder to clarify if one or both of us grew up with parental and/or sibling behaviors which were not okay but were part of everyday life. In such cases, we may not even realize what we are experiencing. Domestic violence, whether physical, emotional or verbal, is about power and control, and the clearer each of us is about boundaries and our own self-respect, the more we will know that we can love the spouse but not allow disrespectful behavior to go unchallenged. Sometimes we may need to seek outside help to change unhealthy patterns.

When considering the usual daily "rub" of two personalities and two sets of preferences and priorities, a sense of humor can go a long way to help us laugh at ourselves and each other. When we were asked at a wedding reception, along with other long-married couples, our secret for a long and happy marriage, both of us recalled the saying at our house, "Yes, dear!"

EVERYWHERE WE LOOK

The more we look at marriage through the lens of asceticism and setting aside of *my way* for *our way*, the more places we can see opportunities to do this. When it comes to parenting or work and money issues, for example, we often internalize our parents' expectations and the ways our parents did things, more than we may realize. Sometimes we're influenced to follow their example, sometimes to live differently. As a couple our challenge is to combine the two sets of attitudes we grew up with to form something that will work for both of us and that places a top priority on our relationship in the midst of all of those demands. Money can be an especially loaded issue as we try to determine, for each of us, what is a need and what is a want. We'll discuss this further when we focus on the topic of discernment.

When it comes to spirituality, whether our religious backgrounds are similar and our traditions are the same or not, each of us has a unique approach. I often tell engaged couples that every marriage is to some extent an interfaith one, because the way I express and grow in my faith and the way you do so are going to be at least somewhat different and may be dramatically so. This gives us plenty of opportunities to exercise an asceticism of encouraging the other person to pray and worship in a way that fits him or her.

The areas for mutual respect and compromise between us are many, but let's explore further two key areas for asceticism in our marriage: communication and fidelity.

CONTINUING TO RISK IN COMMUNICATION

Many of our patterns of couple communication are established by the time of the wedding. We're never really taught how to communicate, except by example, and some of that is far from ideal. Closely related to our communication skills is our ability to trust, and this, also, is heavily influenced by our past experience. Even after many years of marriage the challenge of letting the other person know how we are feeling and thinking does not diminish; it may even increase. Asceticism means that we need to take the time and energy to make that clear to our spouse.

To help the other understand how I am feeling it can be helpful to use an "I-message," perhaps in the form of an X-Y-Z statement like this: In situation X I feel Y because Z. For example: "When we were with your coworkers and their spouses the other night and you told that story about me, I felt embarrassed because I thought it made me look silly in their eyes and I want them to respect me."

By being this specific I have given the other information about how I was feeling and why. I am not demanding that the other change his or her behavior or blaming the other person through a you-message, but I am hoping that my spouse will take my feelings into account in the future. This process is a lot of work and is a very real asceticism, especially when—after we have been married for some years—we hope the other person just knows how we feel.

Drs. John and Julie Gottman, in their work with couples in the Love Lab, which combines both science and relationship skills, found that there are four main blocks in the patterns of marital communication. These can be so toxic that they call them The Four Horsemen of the Apocalypse, after the messengers that bring about the end times in the New Testament book of Revelation. These four blocks are *criticism*, when I attack the other person instead of specific behaviors, *defensiveness*, which denies my responsibility for part of the problem, *contempt* and *sarcasm* which don't fully respect the other person, and *stonewalling*, in which I withdraw and can feel overwhelmed.

It's good to watch out for these destructive tendencies in our interactions as a couple; and they are worth getting help with if they continue to get in the way. The Gottmans suggest that we would do well to aim to make our interactions positive and affirming five times as often as they are critical and negative.

Some of the Gottmans' Four Horsemen can be more common in one gender than in the other. Deborah Tannen, a sociolinguist, pointed out some of the ways that men and women tend to use language differently, which can also affect marital communication. She says that in general women focus on *how* something is being said, the context, while men tend to focus on the *what*, the content, which can make it more likely that men may want to solve the problem, the *what,* rather than just listen to the feelings involved. The goal for each gender also can be different. For men it's often a matter of *competition* or independence in an interaction, where for women the goal is usually *connection*. While these patterns may be gradually changing in our society, they can still impact the ways we are called to asceticism by being open in our communication.

FIDELITY THROUGH THE YEARS

When most of us think of being unfaithful in marriage, sexual infidelity is what comes to mind. But we there are many other ways to be unfaithful. As Paul Simon put it in one of his songs, "There must be fifty ways to leave your lover."

Whenever anything else becomes more important than our relationship, a kind of infidelity occurs. That includes a number of areas in our lives that may not come to mind when we think of being unfaithful, from work to hobbies to the kids. While our careers and our parenting are certainly worthwhile endeavors for the sake of our families, it's far too easy for them to gradually take priority over the two of us. The focus can slip away before we realize it. We may not even see it fully until the kids leave home or one or both of us reaches retirement age.

Psalm 119:2 invites us to seek God with all our heart, and that is what we are called to do with one another: to give *all* our heart, our very selves. There are more and more ways to distract us from each other, many of them connected to the ever-present technology that surrounds us, from video games to social media and even online porn. For many years I taught a university marriage course, and each time I asked students for examples of nonsexual infidelity, I was amazed at the examples they came up with, from being too serious with sports like golf or baseball to too much time with the kids without the spouse. Even working with tools in the shop too much or helping the neighbors so much that one's own family is ignored made their list. We realize now far more than in the past that an emotional affair, even with no sexual involvement, can steal the energy that we should reserve for each other.

Another fact: "Till death do us part" is far longer today than for previous generations due to the increase in our lifespans. This means that the asceticism of putting each other first in our lives is a lifelong, challenging process. Even taking time for a date night with each other involves a kind of asceticism as we choose time as a couple in a busy world.

EVEN EATING?

Asceticism in marriage calls us to share our lives in many ways. There was a little old couple who walked slowly into a fast food restaurant one cold winter evening. They looked out of place among the young families and young couples eating there. Some of the customers looked admiringly at them. You could tell what the admirers were thinking. "Look, there is a couple who has been through a lot together, probably for 60 years or more!" The little old man walked right up to the cash register, placed his order with no hesitation and then paid for the meal. The old couple took a table near the back wall and started taking food from the tray. There was one hamburger, one order of French fries, and one drink. The old man unwrapped the plain hamburger and carefully cut it in half. He placed one half in front of his wife. Then he counted out the French fries, divided them in two piles and neatly placed one pile in front of his wife. He took a sip of the drink, his wife took a sip, and then set the cup down between them. As the man began to eat his few bites of hamburger the crowd began to get restless. Again you could tell what they were thinking. "That poor old couple. All they can afford is one meal for the two of them." As the man began to eat his French fries one young man stood and came over to the old couple's table. He politely offered to buy another meal for the old couple to eat. The old man replied that they were fine. They were used to sharing everything.

Then the crowd noticed that the little old lady hadn't eaten a bite. She just sat there watching her husband eat and occasionally sipping the drink. Again the young man came over and begged them to let him buy them something to eat. This time the lady explained that, no, they were used to sharing everything together. As the old man finished eating and was wiping his face neatly with a napkin the young man could stand it no longer. Again he came over to their table and offered to buy another meal.

After being politely refused again, he finally asked a question of the old lady. "Ma'am, why aren't you eating? You said that you share everything. What is it you're waiting for?" She answered, "It's his turn to use the teeth first!"

❖ ❖ ❖

Although we can laugh at our need to discipline our choices so that we consistently choose each other, it's an important part of our spirituality as a couple. As Damien of Molokai and Thérèse of Lisieux showed us, asceticism is an important part of the spiritual life. As George deals with his reluctance to get up with the baby at night, he can now see how this is just one way that he is called to set aside his own needs for the sake of his marriage and his family. Daily asceticism calls him to be open to further spiritual growth. Next we'll explore how the Incarnation, God being made flesh in Jesus, impacts our marriages.

FOR YOUR REFLECTION:

(After considering these questions individually I encourage you to talk, as a couple, about some or all of them.)

- When it comes to differences between us on punctuality, neatness or planning, the hardest for us to handle has been_____.

- One way that I notice the difference between us in being an extrovert or an introvert is _____.

- When it comes to being morning or evening people we _____.

- At times, it has been hard for me to bring up the topic of_____. For us, an example of the tension between love (generosity) and law (fairness) is _____.

- A difference I've noticed between our spiritual styles is
_____.

- Of the Four Horsemen—criticism, contempt, defensiveness
and withdrawal—the one I see occasionally in our marriage is
_____ . I can see gender differences in our communication when it comes to _____.

Listening to Scripture

Our call to asceticism from Luke's Gospel (17:33):
Whoever seeks to preserve his life will lose it, but
whoever loses it will save it.

FOR FURTHER EXPLORATION

Cloud, Henry, *Necessary Endings: The Employees, Businesses, and Relationships That All of Us Have to Give Up in Order to Move Forward.* Harper Collins, 2010. Explores how to identify and end personal and professional relationships that are no longer life-giving when needed.

Dawes, Gavan, *Holy Man: Fr. Damien of Molokai.* Harper & Row, 1973. A look at a man who gave his whole life to serve those afflicted with leprosy and who was willing to die of it himself.

Gaillardetz, Richard R., *A Daring Promise: A Spirituality of Christian Marriage.* Crossroad, 2002. One of the topics Gaillardetz explores here is conversion and marriage; very connected to asceticism.

Gottman, John M., *The Seven Principles for Making a Marriage Work.* Random House, 2000. Excellent wisdom on the process of marriage from a careful researcher of couples.

Pedersen, Mary Jo, *For Better, For Worse, For God: Exploring the Holy Mystery of Marriage.* Loyola, 2008. Many excellent topics, including forgiveness and reconciliation in marriage.

Thérèse of Lisieux, *The Story of a Soul: The Autobiography of St. Thérèse of Lisieux.* Translated by John Clarke. ICS Publications, 1996. St. Thérèse's account of her life and her "little way."

Viorst, Judith, *Necessary Losses: The Loves, Illusions, Dependencies and Impossible Expectations That All of Us Have to Give Up in Order to Grow.* Simon and Schuster, 1989. Speaking psychologically and personally, the author explores the losses that can help us grow.

Chapter Five

Becoming More Whole
Incarnation in Our Marriage

INCARNATION—UNDERSTANDING THAT GOD BECAME human for us and the implications of that—is a lot to get your head around. It certainly applies to the person of Jesus, but it goes beyond that to help us see all of Creation as drenched with God's presence and love. It helps us to become aware that the human and the spiritual are not two separate realms and can't be separated.

It's essential that we have a basic understanding of this before we try to apply this important and uniquely Christian insight to marriage. For this we look to two figures of the twentieth century who seem to have had little in common but whose lives and vision help us to see the Incarnation at work in the universe and in the neediest of people.

OUR GUIDES: PIERRE TEILHARD DE CHARDIN AND MOTHER TERESA OF CALCUTTA

Jesuit priest Pierre Teilhard de Chardin was a mystic, a philosopher, a scientist and a prophet. He was born in France in an area with plenty of volcanic rocks, which spurred his early interest in geology and paleontology, the study of fossilized animals and plants. He entered the Jesuits at the dawn of the 20th century and pursued his science studies as well as philosophy and theology, later going on to be involved in such projects as the discovery of the remains of Peking Man, then the oldest human ancestor on record.

While he was pursuing these endeavors Fr. Teilhard was also working out a synthesis of the scientific theory of evolution and his own cosmic vision of Christianity. He commented that he wanted to teach people how to see God everywhere, to see God in all that is most hidden, and most substantial in the world. He saw the process of evolution, which resulted in human consciousness, as continuing to unfold, ultimately reaching what he called the Omega Point. He saw this as taking place in Christ, when the spirit of God and the principle of matter were definitively joined. In his "Hymn to Matter," Teilhard sang a blessing to the most fundamental elements on earth, soil and rocks, what he called "mortal matter."

Because his ideas were so far ahead of his time, Teilhard's Jesuit superiors continually refused him permission to publish his ideas, which were little known during his lifetime. At one point he was doing research and field work in China, in a kind of exile, and he wrote about how human beings were helping to extend and consecrate God's creation. When he didn't have the necessary supplies for the Eucharist while on the road, he famously wrote his Mass on the World in which he talked about having the whole earth as his altar and offering there all the labor and suffering of the world..

We're still trying to understand fully Teilhard's vision for us and for the whole of creation, but it has important implications for how we see ourselves and the whole world. Fittingly, Pierre Teilhard de Chardin died on Easter Sunday 1955, pointing us to the way that the Risen Christ is incarnated in all of creation. His writings continue to inspire thinkers to see God at work in the midst of an ever-changing universe.

St. Teresa of Calcutta (now called Kolkata) was born in Albania and for twenty years was a member of a religious community teaching in India when she received what she described as "a call within a call" in the middle of the twentieth century. God, she suddenly realized, wanted something more from her: God wanted her to be poor with the poor and to love him in the disguise of the poorest of the poor.

With the permission of her order she pursued this call, leaving her convent and her religious habit. Wearing a simple white sari with a blue border, she sought out Jesus in the alleyways of the city of Calcutta. She was eventually joined by many of her former students in what came to be known as the Missionaries of Charity, who cared for the sick and unwanted, especially in a home for the dying in Calcutta. Until they died, Mother Teresa and her growing community gave loving care and respect to people who would otherwise die on the streets, helping them to know they were valued and loved as God's precious children. She not only cared for them physically but spiritually, as well.

Mother Teresa's approach was not to change unjust social structures but to provide loving care for those in need. She explained that she and her community were not social workers but contemplatives living in the midst of the world. She said that they were touching the body of Christ twenty-four hours a day. When she was "discovered" by the larger world after having done this work for many years, she didn't allow the fame and public notice to change her, even when she won the Nobel Peace Prize. She said that to show great love for God and neighbor did not require greatness. What mattered was how much love they put into doing what they did.

When visitors would ask to join her in her work, she told them to find their own Calcutta. By saying that she intended to invite others to look at the Incarnation all around them. She said that it was not necessary to search for God in distant lands. Rather, we should look for God nearby, in home, neighborhood, and workplace. Mother Teresa's vision helped many people to see that simply loving another, especially those hard to love, can help address the poverty, material and spiritual, in our world.

Both Pierre Teilhard de Chardin and Mother Teresa can help us see that the Incarnation is not only about Jesus taking on our full humanity long ago; the implications of the Incarnation are strong for how we see the world and the universe around us today and how we see each other as part of the body of Christ. With that in mind, let's explore how the Incarnation is present in our marriages.

SUSAN AND JEFF

Susan smiled as she thought about Jeff's body—and blushed a little, too. She could picture him lying next to her in bed—or even better, on the beach last year when they were on vacation. She still loved his muscular build, and the way he saw and treated her body made her feel more beautiful than she ever felt before. It wasn't as if they had mad, passionate sex all that often, but she just appreciated being able to snuggle next to his solid frame.

Marriage *is* a thing of the body in a way that other ways of life and vocations aren't. And bodies are a part of the Christian tradition in a way that is different than in other religious traditions, although it hasn't often lived up to that heritage, as we'll see. Through the Incarnation, Christians believe that Jesus was God made flesh, that he combined the human and the divine, which changes everything about how we see not only Jesus' body but also our own and others' bodies, not to mention the everyday realities around us, too.

ANCIENT ROOTS

If our bodies *are* good, then how did Susan and Jeff—and most of us—end up with mixed, at times guilt-ridden, reactions to their bodies and sexuality? For the answer we must look back before Christian times to the Ancient Greeks—to the followers of Plato, to be precise. Their view of the human person held reason to be so important and valuable that they saw the spirit/ soul/ mind of the person as more perfect and closer to the divine because it was more reasonable. It was seen to be far higher than the body or flesh, with its tendency to get sick and die, to be smelly and more like the animal realm. The goal for these Neo-platonists was to emphasize the mind and soul and to downplay the body.

This dualistic vision of soul = good and body = bad was in the air as the Christian message was spreading throughout the ancient world. Even though we don't see that dualistic focus if we look in either the Old or New Testaments, before long the thinking in the Christian community became one of getting one's soul to heaven and leaving behind the things of the body. That view included the way sexuality was regarded: as suspect except for the obvious good of children.

But what does all this have to do with us today? We still live with mixed feelings about our sexuality, even many years after the so-called sexual revolution. But it goes beyond just our feelings about sex; we tend to make an implicit distinction between the sacred and the profane, between the holy stuff and ordinary, everyday things. Too often we think of reason and ideas as superior to the important information that our feelings and intuition can also give us, and we fail to see important connections between our feelings and our bodies, and even between stress and illness.

SEEING IN A DIFFERENT WAY

If all this is true, where does the Incarnation—or as one child so aptly put it, Jesus as God's show and tell—fit in here? If Jesus' *whole* self, body included, was holy, then ours is as well. *This* is how we begin to see everything in our lives as grace, as we saw in the first chapter, and to see all that is around us as "sacraments," as visible and tangible ways of experiencing God's love. As early as the first chapter of Genesis we are told that we are made in God's image and likeness, male and female. That longing for one another, Genesis tells us, is of the essence of being made in the image of God. Rather than being *dualistic* and feeling ashamed of part of who we are, we are invited to see ourselves *holistically* and to see that *all* of who we are is called to be holy and whole. The Incarnation helps us to see all of life as holy, even though it's well-disguised most of the time.

To put it another way, John's gospel begins by reminding us that, "In the beginning was the Word, and the Word was with God, and the Word was God . . . And the Word became flesh" (1:1&14). In each marriage the words of the vows exchanged on the wedding day are made flesh every day in the ways that we live out that promise. What we are about, day to day, is becoming one flesh, a unity of two whole persons, which is what man and woman are called to be in Genesis chapter two. (It is important for us to remember that Adam and Eve's shame at their nakedness that we find in chapter three of Genesis is not the way God created the original pair. Rather, it is one consequence of their—and our—own choices and sin.)

OUR WOUNDED SEXUALITY

We usually come to marriage not only with mixed feelings about our own lovability but also about our sexuality. However, this "baggage" isn't helpful when we try to express ourselves authentically to each other, both as new-lyweds and through many years of marriage. Growing up we may inherit a sense that our sexuality and certain parts of our bodies are topics to blush at or to speak of only in hushed tones, or to giggle over. This isn't helpful when our sexuality is a tender and vulnerable part of ourselves to begin with.

Our past sexual experiences also may give us a wariness about giving ourselves too quickly as we may have done when we were young. We may have thought a relationship was true love but it turned out otherwise. Add to this the unrealistic depictions of lovemaking in various media, portrayals which give us unrealistic expectations of what our own sexual experience will be like. Inadvertently or through misguided choices, we may also be affected by the highly damaging effects of online pornography. All this does not add up to a good recipe for sexual health as a couple!

If either or both of us have had any experience of sexual assault or abuse—which is more common than we may realize—this adds to discom-fort or ambivalence when it comes to sexual intimacy in marriage. With past unhealthy sexual experiences, we may need outside help to heal what may stand in the way of our sexual health as a couple. Reading can also be helpful; I often suggest a book to engaged and married couples, *Sheet Music: Uncovering the Secrets of Sexual Intimacy in Marriage*, by Kevin Leman, or something like it. This slim volume can contribute to a more more posi-tive foundation for honest conversations about sexual intimacy and enjoy-ment in marriage. Nobody tells us in advance, for example, that the biggest challenge to sexual intimacy may be trying to stay awake at the end of a full and demanding day! Nor do they mention that when one of us is "in the mood," the other may not be.)

PLEASURE AS KEY AND HOLY

Of all places, in the little-known Old Testament book, the Song of Songs, we see the beauty and goodness of sexual desire described with power and beauty. The lover and beloved, are not identified but are often interpreted as metaphors for God and God's people. The two long for each other with a vivid and sensual desire, even in the first few verses of the book: "Let him kiss me with kisses of his mouth, for your love is better than wine, better than the fragrance of your perfumes" (1:2–3) The Song of Songs reminds us that our passionate longing for our beloved is just a taste of how much God longs for and loves us.

In her article "Why Sex is So Good for Your Marriage," theologian and ethicist Christine Gudorf shows the importance of sexual pleasure in marriage. She declares that good, frequent, mutually pleasurable sex is as important for married couples as is participation in the Eucharist is to membership in the church. She describes sexual loving as central to marriage and that, without it, the relationship may be a close one but it is not marital.

Gudorf sees orgasmic pleasure as the payoff for allowing ourselves to be open and vulnerable, to trust our spouse fully. She even suggests that it's a little taste of God. For many, she continues, the experience of orgasm in a loving marriage is the closest to the divine they have ever been. In this orgasmic experience we feel known to the depth of our souls, loved by one from whom we have no secrets. We feel liberated to risk ourselves and to release consciousness itself. We become totally vulnerable to the loved one. Is there a better way to describe a healthy intimacy with God?

One of the surprising gifts of our lovemaking is just that: making love, creating more love between us. Christine Gudorf comments that sexual desire draws us to sexual intercourse, but sexual desire is also nourished by sexual intercourse.

So too often our sexuality can be an uncomfortable and awkward "language" between us because of so many unhealthy and contradictory messages in our culture. But it can also be an occasion of grace and goodness when we are open to its promise of delight and authentic pleasure.

GOD'S PRESENCE EVERYWHERE

When we begin to look again—to *re-spect*—the world around us differently, with the lens of the Incarnation and the sacramental imagination, we begin to see *everything* as a visible, tangible sign of the invisible, intangible love of God. So, for example, when a married couple first moves in together, they are not just setting up an apartment or a house. They are also creating a space where love dwells and trying to not allow anything to get in the way of that love, such as too much material consumption or media influence. (More about this later.)

We can begin to see hints of this love in the most daily of events, much like the church tradition sees God at work in sharing a meal (Eucharist or communion), washing with water (Baptism), caring for the sick (Anointing of the Sick) and forgiving and seeking reconciliation (Confession.) We don't see this often; it's usually in occasional glimpses and moments. Fr. Ronald Rohlheiser, in his book *The Holy Longing*, talks about the importance of eros, not just as sexual energy but as a deep energy and longing for more life. That's what we are invited to savor in the places we might least expect it.

This vision of seeing all as holy isn't easy to sustain because of the constant busyness and materialism around us which insists instead that life is simply about going to and from work or school, making sure the meals are fixed, getting the laundry clean and being successful. But an incarnational way of seeing knows that the title to this book might well have been *Wholly Together* instead of *Holy Together*. It also understands the title of a talk my husband and I used to give on marital spirituality, which was "Love, Sex, and the Laundry: This is Holy?" Our whole selves, our whole lives—for each of us individually and together as a couple—are important and holy because we are showing forth God in all that we do.

BECOMING ONE FLESH

Becoming one flesh, as we're invited to do in Genesis chapter two, involves not just our sex lives and our bodies, but also our home, our talents and gifts, our careers and volunteer commitments, our relationships and friendships, as well as the ways we take time to appreciate beauty and wonder wherever we are. Let's consider several of these aspects more in detail, starting with our bodies.

From the perspective of the Incarnation we can see more fully what St. Paul tells us when he says that our bodies are temples of the Holy Spirit and that we are members of Christ. That has implications, of course, for how I care for my body: how I nourish myself physically and also "feed" myself with images and ideas, as well as how I keep my body clean and give it enough exercise and rest, not pushing it past its limits. It's important that I not focus too strongly on appearances, my own or others, since we live in a culture that is overly focused on how we look. As I care for myself and those close to me through the challenges of illness and growing older I need to strike a balance between care and attention without over-fixating on my own or another's body. One of the places where much of the care of our bodies takes place is in the bathroom, and sharing a bathroom is often a challenge to a couple's communication skills.

Another important area is gender roles. Spouses may well have grown up with different expectations as to how our own and the opposite gender feels and thinks, behaves, dresses, and takes care of tasks around the house. Because those messages were likely unspoken, they are often more powerful than we expect them to be, even in a time when many limits as to what men and women can or will do are challenged. The more I can be comfortable with who I am as masculine or feminine, and the more I don't allow that to limit me, the better for both of us as a couple. This may well take a significant amount of conversation and sharing, not just initially but at various times in our marriage.

FUTURE GENERATIONS

If we have children or grandchildren, they are, of course, a sort of incarnation of the two of us. As much as we have taught them some lessons about life, about what's important and how to survive and behave, they have certainly taught us a great deal as well.

Their initial complete dependence on us too quickly becomes toddling away from us on unsteady legs and then running and jumping and even pushing the limits of what they have known and been taught. In the process, they teach us to let go and not hold too tightly to what is tenderly close to our hearts. They help us learn to laugh at ourselves as we delight in their discoveries of the amazing world in which we live. As we gaze on them with wonder we are privileged to have a glimpse of how God must regard us every moment of our lives. (I explore these dynamics in far greater detail, especially from a mother's perspective, in *The Liturgy of Motherhood: Moments of Grace*.)

The countless times parents wipe noses and bottoms plunge us, sometimes far more than we would prefer, into an incarnational perspective on the human experience. Most families have stories about some of the earthy accidents and events that happened through the years with infants or teens or even adults. We need to tell these precious extensions of ourselves the amazing stories of when they were born, stories that only we can share with them. These stories are, indeed, a kind of good news in our lives. The nurturing muscles we use as parents and grandparents can also be used in a variety of other ways in our lives, from coaching and mentoring to foster parenting and helping other families in need, whether immigrants or struggling for other reasons. In every giving situation we experience the grace of receiving more than we ever offered the other.

THE DOMESTIC CHURCH

The Second Vatican Council, in the mid-1960s, reminded us of an early Christian insight: that the smallest unit of the church, the community of believers, is not the parish. Even smaller and more basic is the family. And that family begins with the couple. The great Jesuit theologian Father Karl Rahner even wrote that marriage is the smallest form of the church, but a genuine one all the same.

This has important implications for what happens at home, and it's not about setting up pews in the living room. Pope Francis put it clearly and simply when he said that families are authentic domestic churches where we learn tenderness and compassion.

The first book that my husband and I wrote, published in 1984, is titled *Christian Families In the Real World: Reflections On a Spirituality for the Domestic Church.* This book, which is still in print, explores the many implications of the insight that families are domestic churches. Let's explore a couple of the aspects of what this might mean for an incarnational spirituality in the home.

PRAYER AND RITUAL

Marking our days and nights as holy is an important way to remind ourselves that the holy is in our midst. It's important to remember that any prayer and ritual doesn't *make* these times holy; rather, it focuses our attention on what is already holy there. Each household will do this differently, in ways that are comfortable for them, finding the naturally holy times in their unique lives. Let me give some specific examples from our experience, not because they are ideal or a model but merely as illustrations.

Evening meal time is marked at our house with a meal prayer accompanied by a lit candle in the middle of the table with the other lights turned off. We begin with the sign of the cross followed by holding hands as we pray. This reminds us that the light of Christ is in our midst whenever two or more are gathered. Depending on the season, we may pray the standard grace ("Bless us, O Lord, and these thy gifts . . .") or we may sing part of a seasonal song, like "O Come, O Come Emmanuel" during Advent. When our sons were at home they would sometimes take turns choosing what the grace would be, which led to some unique variations.

Important holidays might include special meal prayers and guests around our table. Some families use two candles at these times, which we never did, but the first one can be lit in gratitude for the all the graces and blessings of the past and the second one in hope for all that the future holds. (Many ideas about how to use these can be found in *The Blessing Candles* by Gaynell Bordes Cronin and Jack Rathschmidt.) Some families use a red plate, on which is inscribed, "You are special today," to mark the birthdays, anniversaries and other milestones in the home.

Preparing for bed and sleep is also a naturally holy time, one in which we can easily see the strong, innate sense of ritual that young children have. Parents and babysitters alike can testify that there is a "proper" way that a story, a stuffed animal friend and a sip of water happen at bedtime, and for children the "proper" routine definitely needs to be followed. Besides night prayers and a story, this seemed to be a natural time for our three sons to reflect on their days and to raise heavy, thoughtful questions—just when the parent wanted to be able to rest at the end of a long day!

Blessings were important in our house when our children were younger, both daily and for special occasions. We gave each one a nightly blessing when tucking them into bed, signing them with a cross on their forehead while saying, "God bless you; have a peaceful night." Whenever anyone was going on a trip, this called for a blessing, too, and as our sons grew sometimes the blessing they might give us before our trips was courtesy of the "Star Wars" movies: "May the Force be with you." Through the years we have blessed a new house, a new car, even the riding toys when our sons were young, after which they wheeled happily away. We had a blessing before the first day of school each year and partied gratefully after a blessing at graduations, too.

Each season had its own reasons for celebration, from carving pumpkins to coloring eggs to even the time when we did our own Stations of the Cross. Because our oldest, who was then in kindergarten, had seen a reenactment of Jesus being condemned to die and nailed to the cross at his school, he wanted to do it at home. So we found a plastic hammer for pronouncing Jesus guilty and later for nailing him to a cross, which was formed by two sticks tied together. We had a hand towel from the kitchen for Veronica to wipe the face of Jesus, and even a large pillow tomb where we buried Jesus and came back to find that he'd risen from the dead! Their need to pray with their bodies taught us a lot about how these preschool children—and perhaps the rest of us—need to use our bodies more than we sometimes think to do.

HOSPITALITY: WELCOMING THE STRANGER

Although we don't have guests in our home nearly as often as some families do, we are aware that welcoming others into our home is a holy experience. Whether guests are simply there to share a meal or are staying in our home overnight or for a few weeks, they are a special grace. In the New Testament's Letter to the Hebrews the author reminds both the first-century Christians, who had a strong tradition of Middle-Eastern hospitality, and us, "Do not neglect hospitality, for through it some have unknowingly entertained angels."(13:2)

Welcoming others into our home or giving shelter to those who may need a meal or a place to stay for a while is an important way of welcoming Christ into our everyday lives, sharing what we have with those whose paths cross ours. This is incarnational spirituality at work and also a way of evangelization, of sharing the gospel message that all are loved and accepted, not just through words but by the way that takes shape in our home.

❖ ❖ ❖

The more Susan reflects on how the love that she and Jeff have for each other is a thing of the body, the more she can see that it does not mean that it isn't spiritual. In fact, their love is whole and holy, embracing every aspect of their life together and helping them to see holiness in places they might not have suspected it to be—just as Pierre Teilhard de Chardin helped us to see it in the whole universe and Mother Teresa helped us to see it in the lowly and dying in Calcutta. Susan is beginning to appreciate more fully how both she and Jeff are an important part of the larger Body of Christ. Next we turn to considering the choices we make in our marriages.

FOR YOUR REFLECTION

(After considering these questions individually I encourage you to talk, as a couple, about some or all of them.)

- One way in which I have mixed feelings about my body is. . . .

- In caring for my body I often feel. . ..
- How well have we expressed our love and affection physically?
- Is our sexuality an area we can talk about comfortably? If not, what might help that?
- Are we each comfortable with how we express our love physically?
- A past experience that has impacted our sense of the goodness of sexuality and pleasure is _____.
- A challenge for us when it comes to gender roles has been _____.
- If we've had children, how have they helped us see our life and love more holistically?
- One thing our children have taught us is _____.
- When I think about our home as a domestic church, I . . .
- One of our everyday experiences that strikes me as especially holy is . . .
- I like the way we have celebrated _____ in our home.

> ### Listening to Scripture
> *The importance of the body from the First Letter To the Corinthians (6:19–20):*
>
> Do you not know that your body is a temple of the holy Spirit within you, whom you have from God, and that you are not your own? . . . Therefore glorify God in your body.

FOR FURTHER EXPLORATION

Cronin, Gaynell and Rathschmidt, Jack, *The Blessing Candles: 58 Simple Mealtime Prayer-Celebrations.* St. Anthony Messenger Press, 2000. Helpful ideas for simple rituals at home to mark important days.

Egan, Eileen, *Such a Vision of the Street.* Doubleday, 1985. A clear portrait of St. Teresa of Calcutta by a woman who worked with her for many years.

Finley, Kathleen, *The Liturgy of Motherhood: Moments of Grace.* Sheed & Ward, 2004. Based on the liturgical year, an exploration of mothers' and women's spirituality.

Savoring God: Praying With All Our Senses. Ave Maria Press, 2003. Helpful ideas in praying with everyday objects and seeing the holy in the ordinary.

More Savoring God: Praying With All Our Senses. Resource Publications, 2012. More of the same.

Finley, Mitch and Kathy, *Christian Families in the Real World: Reflections On a Spirituality for the Domestic Church.* Wipf and Stock, 2018. This book explores the implications of seeing families as the domestic church.

Hays, Edward, *Pray All Ways: A Book for Daily Worship Using All Your Senses.* Forest of Peace Books, 1981. A serious and playful look at a variety of ways to pray with our bodies.

King, Ursula, *Spirit of Fire: The Life and Vision of Teilhard de Chardin.* Orbis, 1996. A helpful and clear look at the life, work and accomplishments of Fr. Teilhard.

Leman, Kevin, *Sheet Music: Uncovering the Secrets of Sexual Intimacy in Marriage.* Tyndale House, 2003. A faith-based look at the grace of married sexuality.

Penner, Clifford and Joyce, *The Gift of Sex: A Guide to Sexual Fulfillment.* Thomas Nelson, 2003. More help in seeing how our sexuality is a gift from God.

Chapter Six

Choosing with Care
Discernment in our Marriage

IN MAKING THE SMALL and large decisions that make up our lives, many of us don't stop to think about what we're deciding and how we do so. The process of discernment helps us to make significant life choices mindfully and in light of our faith. Before we take a look at how this might take shape in marriage we need to understand more fully what discernment is—and is not. For that we turn to two giants of our faith, living at different times in history, who embodied the process of discernment themselves and taught others how to listen for God's presence in the midst of their own lives.

OUR MODELS: ST. IGNATIUS OF LOYOLA AND HILDEGARD OF BINGEN

Inigo Lopez de Loyola was born in the Basque region of present-day Spain, into a noble family, and was fascinated, as were most boys and young men of that era, with honor and chivalry. In 1521, trying to unsuccessfully defend the city of Pamplona from attack, he was struck in the leg by a cannonball, causing a significant injury followed by several painful operations and a prolonged convalescence. During the time he was laid up, Ignatius wanted to read the chivalrous romances of the time that he admired, but all that was available to him were books on the lives of Jesus and of the saints. The more he read such books, the more the idea grew in him that he could be dedicated to God's service, not that of the king, and that completely changed his life direction.

Later, he would formulate this service in his prayer known as the *Suscipe*:

> Take, Lord, and receive all my liberty, my memory, my under-standing, and my entire will, all I have and call my own. You have given all to me. To you, Lord, I return it. Everything is yours; do with it what you will. Give me only your love and your grace, that is enough for me.

Ignatius spent several months in solitary reflection and prayer and went on a couple of pilgrimages, traveling in search of where he was called to be. When it became clear in prayer that he should become a priest, he resumed his education and eventually recruited several of his fellow students in Paris to form a new religious order to serve the church in any way that might be needed. They became known as the Society of Jesus , or Jesuits. The needs of the church at that time were many, as it was reeling from the challenge of the Protestant Reformation and was trying to find its place in the expanding exploration of new parts of the world, especially in Asia and the Americas. The Jesuits were seen as men of learning as well as action, and although they had a special vow to put themselves at the service of the pope, they found themselves in the midst of controversy at times, as did Ignatius himself.

One of St. Ignatius' big contributions to the church was the method of formation for the Jesuits, the Spiritual Exercises, designed initially to be followed in a thirty-day retreat. The Spiritual Exercises helped retreatants to pray with Scripture in guided meditation. It also helped with discernment, the process of listening in faith for God's voice in the midst of life. Ignatius urged his followers to act as if everything depended on them, but trust as if everything depended on God.

Today Jesuits are educators, pastors, and spiritual directors all over the world, helping people to understand how to serve God in their own unique ways. Many still find Ignatius' insights on discernment helpful when making important life decisions.

While she was born in an earlier time, Hildegard of Bingen was a truly remarkable woman for any age, and certainly for the twelfth century in which she lived, one which was not used to seeing women in prominent roles. Not only was she an abbess and founder of a Benedictine community, but she was also a musician and composer, poet and artist, physician and pharmacist, author, theologian, and preacher. From an early age she was raised by a hermitess who helped prepare her for the Benedictine life, which she entered at age eighteen.

Gradually, it came to light that Hildegard had vivid visions beginning at the age of three. When she became prioress these visions were written down with the approval of the local church authorities. She later would travel, preaching throughout the area; she also corresponded with many officials of the time, sharing her spiritual insights but also criticizing them when she thought it necessary.

Key to her visions was an understanding of the cosmos as a whole and our role within it. She saw humanity as having in itself the entire cosmos, indeed, all of creation. Hildegard's use of herbs in medicine and physiology seems to have anticipated the principles of homeopathy. She also composed hauntingly beautiful and original music; she saw music as re-establishing the harmony that Satan had disturbed.

When it comes to our choices and discernment, then, we need to act in harmony with God, she explained. Above all, for Hildegard this involves a deep appreciation for justice and for all creation, and in that respect she clearly predates the modern ecological awareness. If we fall in love with creation, she said, then we will respond to its endangerment with full hearts

As we humans operate as the thinking heart of the universe, Hildegard said, we may at times generate controversy, as she did. For example, she found herself in trouble late in her life for allowing a young man who had been excommunicated—cut off from the church and the sacraments—to be buried in the monastery cemetery. Her reason was that she insisted that he had been reconciled to the church before his death. But the bishop sanctioned the convent nonetheless, and she protested bitterly. Soon after the interdict was lifted she died in 1179.

Hildegard leaves much for us to consider in our own choices, especially her vision that everything is saturated with connectedness and relatedness.

Both Ignatius of Loyola and Hildegard of Bingen help us to see that our decisions are not just a private matter but are part of our relationship to God, to the wider community of faith, and even to the whole universe. Making those decisions thoughtfully and prayerfully is not just helpful for us but for all of creation. Let us now turn to consider how discernment can take place in marriage.

DENNIS AND KAREN

As their anniversary drew near, Dennis found himself reflecting on some of the choices that he and Karen had made through the years. There were the easier ones, like moving back to be close to their extended families as the kids came along, and then some of the harder ones, involving their jobs, their educations, and some health issues they had to deal with a few years ago.

As they prepared for their wedding, those many years ago, Dennis realized, neither of them thought they would face as many choices as they had. Thankfully, he realized that most of the time they had been in agreement about the important values to consider in almost any choice they had to make. Like Dennis and Karen's lives, our lives can be seen as a pattern, a tapestry of the choices we have made throughout our days. The great majority of those choices we make without much thought, just going through the everyday motions. But the major choices in our lives help shape who we are and deserve significant attention. One way to be intentional about making these life decisions is discernment.

WHAT IS DISCERNMENT?

Discernment refers to the process of considering and sifting the variety of motives and energies that lead to each of our decisions, usually based on more than just our feelings in the moment. St. Ignatius of Loyola, the founder of the Jesuits, invites us to stop and listen to what's happening within us and how God might be a part of that experience, especially in terms of what we want most deeply and where we find the greatest energy and life.

Fr. Henri Nouwen, a spiritual master of our time, described this process as listening and responding to that place within us where our deepest desires join hands with God's desire. As discerning people, we examine our impulses, motives, and options to learn which will lead us closer to God and compassion for ourselves and other people, and which ones lead us further away. Gradually, we realize that what previously seemed so important loses its power over us. Our desire to be successful, well liked and influential becomes increasingly less important as we grow in our understanding of how close God is to each one of us.

This approach may sound daunting and beyond our abilities, but let's see how this might impact some of the main decisions that come along in marriage. First, we'll explore some of the choices couples make and then how we might be more intentional about making those decisions.

OUR CHOICES

Long before a man and woman meet as prospective spouses, each has made choices that has shaped his or her life in important ways. Often we're not aware of the pattern we weave with those choices, but others can see the pattern more clearly than we can. It is more apparent to us when we come to the key choices along the way: Where do I go to school? Where do I live? What job do I take? How do I spend my money? But it is also reflected in our daily patterns: What do I eat? What do I wear? What kind of car do I drive? With whom do I associate and have as friends?

When another important person comes into my life, this presents more choices. Do I want to pursue a relationship with this person? Is this someone I may want to marry and spend my life with? Should we live together before marriage?

Sometimes I ask engaged couples with whom I work why they broke off serious relationships or engagements in the past. They often reply that their lives and the choices each of them made, didn't seem to connect well with the life of the other person; their "tapestries" didn't overlap well.

If we do mesh well as a couple, then we are confronted with another series of choices: When and where will we marry? Where will we live and how will we support ourselves, including any education or training? Are we going to be emotionally and geographically close to both our families? To one or to neither? What friends do we want to surround us as a couple and as a family? Do we begin a family right away, wait for later or choose not to have children?

As the years go by, some of the choices we face are predictable, such as schooling for any children we have or what to do when it comes to retirement. Others aren't so expected, such as major health issues for one of us or a family member.

DIFFERENCES BETWEEN US

The process we use to make these choices may vary considerably between us, both in the how and the what. It can vary in the *how* in that one of us may be more eager to decide quickly and perhaps spontaneously, whereas the other wants to weigh the possibilities carefully, perhaps consulting others before making a choice.

We may also differ when it comes to the *what,* the values we weigh in making a decision, which in turn is related to some of what we explored about vocation in an earlier chapter. Our preferences may not be the same when it comes to the following: Do we value privacy and isolation over connection with each other and others? Is it more important where we live or what we are each doing in our careers? Do we value status, getting ahead and competition over compassion and charity? When it comes to friends and connections, are they important for status or for their own sake? How important are appearances to each of us over a deeper, unique beauty in each person? What about the latest conveniences and gadgets over a simpler way of life? How, if at all, does respect for the earth play a role when it comes to our own convenience and comfort? And where does our faith come into play in the values and goals that we consider in making our choices?

One of the ways that the differences in our values may take shape is in our attitudes toward money and spending. Money may mean different things to each of us—for example, security vs. freedom—and our spending at times may not be reasonable. It can be helpful for couples to decide on an amount above which neither of them will spend without checking in with the other, thus acknowledging that this is *our* money and the choices about to spending it should be ours together.

If and when we have children, our choices become more complex, knowing that what we decide can impact them for the rest of their lives. One of the most important decisions is how we discipline them, remembering that the word *discipline* implies teaching them to make good choices for themselves, not just settling for *punishing* them, which may only motivate them to avoid the punishment in the future. With children in the picture, all our decisions as a couple are no longer about only the two of us, they are also about teaching values by the most effective means: the way we model them ourselves.

THE MOMENTUM OF OUR CHOICES

Like it or not, there's an energy, a momentum in our choices; if not in each particular one, then certainly in the pattern and network of them. Our choices not only indicate which direction we tend, but they also nudge us further in that direction.

The poet Robert Frost spoke to that dynamic in his well-loved poem, "The Road Not Taken." After describing the two paths and which one he had chosen, Frost remarks that he reserved the first path for sometime in the future. Yet knowing how unpredictable life can be, he doubts that he will ever return to this place where the two paths separate. Then he adds that having taken the path he did made all the difference in his life.

C. S. Lewis, in *Mere Christianity*, points out how such choices begin to shape us. Each and every time a person makes a choice, he says, he or she changes the center of his or her being into something somewhat different than it was before.

When I taught university students, I often marveled at how little they realized that the choices they made at this point in their lives would influence everything in the future in ways they could not begin to imagine.

THE PROCESS OF DISCERNMENT

When faced with a decision, whether we're aware of how it may impact our future or not, some steps may be helpful to consider as we make that choice. There are many resources on discernment available. For example, in her book *Hearing with the Heart: A Gentle Guide to Discerning God's Will for Your Life*, Debra Farrington explores a process based on the insights of St. Ignatius Loyola.

Besides bringing a prayerful awareness to the whole endeavor, the first step is to be clear on the question that you're trying to discern. This isn't as obvious as it might seem; sometimes what we thought we might be considering isn't the real question at all. For example, what may look like a matter of whether I should stay at this particular job or not may in fact open up the question of whether this is what I want to be doing with my life at all. And so the options begin to be clearer as I clarify the question itself.

The next move is to try to be as open and objective about the outcome as possible, which is also easier said than done. I often describe it as being equally balanced on both feet so that we can be open to whatever becomes clear as the process unfolds, knowing that whatever God wants for me and for us is what we want to choose. And praying for God's guidance is clearly what we need to do next.

But God wants us to use our reasoning skills, so this is where a good old pros-and-cons list can come in handy. Farrington suggests some helpful questions to then consider:

> What will be gained in choosing each of the paths before you?
> What will be lost by rejecting any of the choices?
> How do the choices benefit others?
> In what ways do the choices inconvenience or disrupt the lives of others?
> What excites you most about the options? What do you look forward to?
> What would you dislike if you picked one path or the other?
> What are your motivations for choosing one option or another?

The more honest we can be with ourselves and each other, the sooner we get to what is most important to us and our real motivation in making this decision. This is a time to use our reason as an important gift that God gives us and also to listen deep inside to what seems to give us the most peace and the least turmoil.

Perhaps there's one option that may seem overwhelming to consider, such as changing a profession or adopting a child. It may be helpful to break such a choice down into specific steps to see what it might entail to pursue it and who or what you might need to consult first.

If time allows, one of the most helpful tools can be to consult our feelings. If you have the possibilities narrowed down to two or even three options, then you can give yourself a couple of days to make the decision one way and then decide the other way for the same amount of time. Meanwhile, you're listening inside for what Ignatius calls consolation or desolation, since he says that the Holy Spirit doesn't work in turmoil but in peace. Consolation is a deep peace and joy that pulls you toward the love of God and God's peace, perhaps with renewed energy, and a release of tension that you've been holding in your body. Desolation may show itself as turmoil, inner disquiet and anxiety, even unhappiness and boredom. These feelings are tricky to read in ourselves at times, and often a trained spiritual director or guide should be consulted. (One source of help in finding a spiritual director can be Spiritual Directors International, www.sdicompanions.org.)

DECIDING AS A COUPLE

Making a decision well and prayerfully as an individual is hard enough, but doing so as a couple is even more challenging. We each need to listen to our deepest selves, as well as to the well-being of the other and the deepest good for us as a couple. In order to do this well, we need times of solitude individually, as well as time as a couple.

The decisions to be made can seem endless some days, but let's consider three specific challenges. The first of these surrounds us every day: technology. From the TV we probably grew up with to the personal computer, and the amazing tool that is the smart phone in our pockets or purses, technology continues to grow more sophisticated and more invasive in our lives. We may not know how we would operate without today's technology.

It certainly can help keep us stay connected through texting and other means. But it also can powerfully distract and distance us from one another. If we don't make decisions about whether "screens" are allowed at the table, or in bed, we have decided by omission to allow the seductive nature of technology to take over our attention and our time with one another. This can be an area where we may not agree, whether it has to do with social media or video games or watching sports or whatever.

Attitudes toward nature and the amount of time we spend there can be another challenging area as a couple. Do we each equally enjoy being in a natural setting, whether that's stargazing on a clear night or camping or hiking or the many other options? Are we both as aware of what we consume and about recycling, as well as attempts to cut down on packaging as it impacts the environment? These concerns and interests can be hard to communicate about and explain to each other.

This brings up a third challenge for a couple: handling differences and conflict between us. When we disagree, and one of us wins and one of us loses, in a way we both lose, even if the "loser" has a turn next time to "win." Even if we're not all that competitive, the one who loses may still be looking for a chance to level the playing field. The reality is that none of us grew up learning how to achieve a win/win situation, even though that's what our marriage really needs to thrive. The more we can find a way that works for both of us, the more we're helping our children and our world begin to learn a new way of coming together in a peaceful way rather than in the anger and violence that we see so frequently around us.

❖ ❖ ❖

Dennis can now see that the choices he and Karen made through the years and the way they made those decisions, helped weave a rich and satisfying life together. Just as Ignatius Loyola and Hildegard of Bingen had to make some difficult and life-changing choices, so have they. He is confident as they face the future together that they have the tools they need to make good, thoughtful, prayerful decisions. Next we turn to how dying and rising happens over and over in our marriage.

FOR YOUR REFLECTION:

(After considering these questions individually I encourage you to talk about some or all of them as a couple.)

- What are some of the main choices that we have made in our lives and how have they helped shape who we are?

- Which were the hardest to make? Which were relatively easy?

- One of the biggest differences between us when it comes to making decisions is _____.

- If we could go back and change one choice we made, what would it be and why?

- I remember how challenging it was to make the decision to _____.

- What are the choices that we are most proud of, and why?

- I'm so glad we decided to _____ .

- Right now or soon we're going to need to decide what to do about

_____ .

Listening to Scripture

God's reply to King Solomon, who could ask God for anything at all, from I Kings (3:11–12):

Because you asked for this—you did not ask for a long life for yourself, nor for riches, nor for the life of your enemies—but you asked for discernment to know what is right— I now do as you request. I give you a heart so wise and discerning that there has never been anyone like you until now, nor after you will there be anyone to equal you.

FOR FURTHER EXPLORATION

Bowie, Fiona and Oliver Davis, eds., *Hildegard of Bingen: Mystical Writings.* Crossroad, 1995. A good introduction to Hildegard's writings and their amazing scope.

Farrington, Debra K., *Hearing With the Heart: A Gentle Guide to Discerning God's Will for Your Life.* Jossey-Bass, 2003. The author leads us through a helpful process for discovering how to invite God's presence into every aspect of our daily lives.

Nouwen, Henri, *Discernment: Reading the Signs of Daily Life.* Harper One, 2013. The collected ideas of a powerful spiritual teacher on how to listen more carefully to our lives.

Silf, Margaret, *Wise Choices: A Spiritual Guide to Making Life's Decisions.* BlueBridge, 2007. A gentle, poetic look at the process of choosing with wisdom.

Tetlow, Joseph, *Ignatius Loyola: Spiritual Exercises with Commentary.* Crossroad, 2009. A helpful introduction to St. Ignatius' vision and gift to the church of the Spiritual Exercises.

Chapter Seven

Stronger and Deeper
Dying and Rising in our Marriage

DYING AND RISING SOUNDS pretty serious — as well as being something that we associate with Jesus but not so much with anyone else, let alone ourselves. We may have some challenges in our lives, individually and as a couple, but we wouldn't necessarily call it dying and rising. As we take a closer look, however, we'll see that we do die and rise in all kinds of ways. These ways may not be apparent at first but they are part of our experience, even on a daily basis.

To take a closer look at this idea we'll focus on two men from different Christian backgrounds in the twentieth century who faced extremely difficult moral and political situations. We'll consider how their dying and rising can shed light on our own. Many would consider both these men to be martyrs, those who die for their faith.

OUR MODELS: DIETRICH BONHOEFFER
AND ST. OSCAR ROMERO

Dietrich Bonhoeffer was a Lutheran pastor and theologian in 1930s Germany, watching with horror his country follow the Nazi regime with its hatred and anti-Semitism. He helped found the Confessing Church, a group of pastors and seminarians opposing Hitler and insisting on the independence of the churches.

69

As the situation in his homeland worsened, Bonhoeffer turned his back on the prospect of teaching safely in New York to return to his country and get involved with the Abwehr, the German Military Intelligence. There he and others were involved with a secret military conspiracy to overthrow the government. When their plot was discovered and investigated they were imprisoned, and on April 9, 1945—just two weeks before American troops liberated the area—Bonhoeffer was hanged with five others in the group.

Although he was only thirty-nine at the time of his death, Pastor Bonhoeffer had been reflecting for many years on how to live in faith. The ultimate question for a responsible person, he said, is not how to escape danger but how the coming generation can live its faith. For Bonhoeffer this came straight from his writings and teaching, which took Christian faith to the center of life, not staying on its edges. He saw following Christ as a matter of engagement in the world, living unreservedly life's ups and downs. By doing this, he said, we abandon ourselves into the loving arms of God, joining Christ in his suffering and death. That, he said, is genuine faith.

Because Bonhoeffer saw faith at the center of life, he chose to die long before he was put to death, thus to live a more full life in Christ. He rejected a church that was remote or removed from daily life, but rather embraced what he called "religionless Christianity," using a different kind of language in a world that he could see was rapidly changing. His writings and thought continues to live on to inspire people of faith today.

Archbishop Oscar Romero found himself in a similarly challenging situation in El Salvador, although when he was named to head the Catholic Church in that country he was not seen as someone who would challenge the status quo. But soon after becoming a bishop he had to officiate at the funeral of his friend, Jesuit priest Rutilio Grande, who was assassinated as a result of his commitment to social justice for the poor. That event seemed to change the archbishop, and he began to speak out in his weekly radio addresses about human rights, especially those of the poor.

This put him in conflict with the fourteen ruling families of the country, who were nominally Catholic, and yet the military and death squads directed by them were attempting to scare the poor into submission and silence. But for Romero, today officially a saint, a church that does not unite itself with the poor, in order to denounce the injustice committed against, them is not truly the church of Jesus Christ.

As the chaos in his country continued to grow, Archbishop Romero spoke out more and more forcefully in his radio sermons, causing some to say that he was subordinating the gospel to politics. The day before his death he appealed directly to members of the military, begging them to refuse illegal orders and to stop the repression. The next day he was shot while celebrating Mass in a hospital chapel and died within minutes. He had clearly considered what his fate might be. A couple of weeks before his assassination he commented in an interview that he had often been threatened with death. However, he said, he did not believe in death but in the resurrection. If his enemies killed him, Archbishop Romero said, he would rise again in the Salvadoran people.

Both Dietrich Bonhoeffer and Oscar Romero suffered death in difficult situations, more than most of us will ever face. Both had already died to the comfort of not challenging the way things were in their world. They also said far more about life and hope by how they died than most of us will with our whole lives. The paradox is that, like Jesus, in their dying began their rising, as we will now explore in the experience of marriage.

DEBBIE AND PETER

Debbie was grateful and pleased when she thought about how she and Peter had handled their problems over the past nine months. She had watched Peter go from insisting that there wasn't any difficulty between them to realizing that they had some issues to work on to reluctantly deciding that they needed help in order to sort out their feelings and perceptions as the kids were leaving home.

When she thought about the process they had gone through, it reminded her of when her mother had died a couple of years ago. As her mother's health had gotten worse, she and her siblings realized that the end was drawing near and that they could prepare for it by beginning to say goodbye in anticipation of the loss of their mom.

For Peter and her, first there was some grieving needed for the ideal marriage with few problems they thought they had and were leaving behind. And gradually, after realizing they had work to do, there was the beginning of something new, which was different and still somewhat unfamiliar, but now they were learning how to live in a new way with the help of their marriage counselor.

DYING AND RISING: THE PASCHAL MYSTERY

What Debbie saw and reflected on is the kind of dying and rising to new life that happens over and over in our lives. Sometimes that experience is more difficult than at other times, but it always leads to new life if we can be open to the process.

The theological term for that dying and rising, especially in Jesus' life, is the Paschal Mystery. Jesus' death on Good Friday was not the end of the story; it was part of a bigger story of his resurrection on Easter Sunday.

Just as Jesus needed to die in order to rise again, the Christian perspective sees that dying and rising is something that we're *all* called to and, further, that the new life, the rising, already begins *in the midst of* the dying, although it rarely seems like it at the time. In fact, the *dying* is the beginning of new possibility and growth, the *rising*, that might not have happened without that experience. Let's take a closer look.

ATTITUDES IN OUR CULTURE

As we consider dying and rising it's important to remind ourselves that we live in the midst of a culture that would rather not look at or talk about death. Rather than people dying at home as they did in the past, most are in a hospital or hospice facility for their last days. Then, unlike many cultures in the world that prepare the body at home for burial we "farm that out" to professional morticians. We don't even like to say the word "death;" we'd rather use a euphemism than to say a person died. We say that someone "departed" or "passed away," or Grandma "went to her reward" or is "no longer with us." Rarely do we say that someone died.

There have been some advances in our attitudes toward death in recent years, such as Elizabeth Kubler Ross reminding us in the late 1960s that death and grief is a process, with identifiable stages of denial, anger, bargaining, depression and, finally, acceptance. The Hospice movement has also helped many families see death in a new and powerful way. But, by and large, our culture would rather medicate and ignore both pain and death as much as possible.

Death, of course, is not only unavoidable; it's necessary. The theologian Rosemary Radford Ruether reminds us to look again at dying, especially in the natural world around us. "In nature, death is not an enemy but a friend of the life process. The death side of the life cycle is an essential component of that renewal of life by which dead organisms are broken down and become the nutrients of new organic growth."

TRANSITIONS IN OUR LIVES

Although the dying and rising that we're considering here happens often, even daily, it's perhaps easiest to see it when we look at the major transitions that happen in our lives. William Bridges, in his helpful book *Transitions:*

Making Sense of Life's Changes, says that in any life transition there are three basic parts, which he calls Endings, the Neutral Zone and The New Beginning. I have found it helpful to name them slightly differently, but the dynamics are the same. What I would call Separation—and he would call Endings—marks a situation when, either through my own choice or because of circumstances beyond my control, I find myself pulling away from the way things have been in my life. It may be the end of a school year, a graduation, the final days of a job or or even of a particular time in our marriage; something pulls me away from the status quo, from the comfort of what I know. Bridges talks about four "d"s here: *disengagement* from the way things have been, *disidentification* as I see myself in a new light, *disenchantment* as I look around me with new eyes, and *disorientation* because I'm not fully sure what lies ahead.

The second stage of a life transition is the most important part. Bridges calls this the Neutral Zone, and I call it Marginality; this is a time when I'm no longer in the old way of doing things but I'm not yet fully in the new. This is uncomfortable, a time of vulnerability and risk, without familiar markers or much clarity. I like to picture it as a narrow, dark passage with a lack of clear light at the end of the tunnel. All I know when I'm there is what I *don't* know, and I'm not sure when life will become clear. It's especially hard to pray. One of the helpful suggestions he makes in order to manage at this point is to spend reflective time in solitude to gain perspective.

Whether or not we take that break to consider what's happening, gradually in our life passage some light and clarity begins to emerge, and what Bridges calls A New Beginning, and what I call Re-integration, begins to happen. Gradually I gain my bearings and find that I know what I'm doing again. What emerges from this process does not look like what came before; life has now changed. Some call this outcome the new normal.

Let's take a look at these stages in Debbie and Peter's experience. The separation came with the realization that the ways that they have been relating to each other were not working as well as they once did. Also, it's not unusual for that realization to be clearer for one spouse earlier than for the other. Marginality begins with the question of what they they can do about what's changing, including the option to see a marriage therapist. As they clarify what led to the change and the ways they might live differently now as a couple, some re-integration is evident.

A NEVER-ENDING STREAM

When we look more closely at the transitions in our lives, we begin to see that this process is happening one way or other most of the time. Something is always changing in our marriage; we are indeed *marrying* each other, not just *married*. The changing and dying and rising begins early and continues in countless ways, from revising our first expectations as we met and got married, to the wedding and honeymoon plans, to early homes we had, our roles as spouses, and the illnesses or needs of other family members.

Children, of course, bring a different set of transitions, from formerly being childless to being the three of us, and then perhaps more. The experience of dying and rising is constant with kids, with the milestones that seem to take forever with the first child and then happen rapidly with successive offspring. The infant becomes the toddler who becomes the grade schooler and then preteen, teen and young adult, more quickly than we ever expected. Children's injuries, illnesses or other crises are tough for us to watch, and we would rather take them on ourselves than watch our youngsters suffer.

Then there's the challenge of watching young adults cope with difficulties we wish we could protect them from. In the midst of all this is the challenge to accept the little death of giving up trying to be a perfect spouse or parent. But we do this so that we might welcome the "resurrection" of knowing that we bring our loving, generous, flawed selves to both tasks.

THREE SIGNIFICANT CHALLENGES

Three major issues that can arise in a marriage challenge our ability to die and rise with Christ and to see the paschal mystery of Jesus at work in our lives. These are the deaths of parents or other family members, an empty nest and/or retirement, and the possibility of divorce.

Many couples say that, for many reasons, the death of a parent presented more difficulties in their marriage than they expected. These include the unique ways in which each spouse grieves, the family dynamics that come to the surface in that situation, and the difficulties that can surface in trying to make arrangements for the surviving parent or the estate. The other spouse can only stand by and be supportive as these family events unfold. Some of these same dynamics can also happen in the excruciating experience of the death of a child.

The process of launching young adult children can be particularly complicated these days, but when that finally happens and the home is quiet again, many couples, like Peter and Debbie, face a new challenge: how to be a couple without the shared project of being parents in the same way as before. The freedom that opens up for both spouses is both exciting and strange and only expands with retirement for one or both of them.

Retirement is a relatively recent challenge for couples. As our health care resources and longevity continue to improve we are able to be healthier and live longer than previous generations. Although it can be tricky, as one spouse often retires before the other, eventually we are faced with more time with each other. Couples who navigate this dying and rising especially well tend to have activities, whether part-time work, hobbies, or volunteer efforts that keep them active and give them a meaningful time structure so that the other spouse doesn't need to be everything for them. They may find that some volunteer activities or travel together helps also. For couples in this situation it might be more appropriate to talk about redirection rather than retirement.

Besides the death of a spouse, which we will consider later, the possible experience of divorce is one of the hardest experiences of dying and rising in a marriage. Even in situations of abuse or mental illness, no one likes to see the dissolution of the hopes that a couple had for sharing their lives together. When spouses have tried to reconcile, with outside help, and have been unsuccessful, the dying is evident to all concerned, even friends, but the rising is far harder to identify.

SIX STATIONS OF DIVORCE

Researcher Paul Bohannon described six stations, or experiences, that happen in the process of any divorce, although not in any particular order. Listen to the dying—and possible rising—at work in each of them, perhaps in a couple you may know who has gone through this experience.

In the *emotional divorce* the spouses gradually grow apart from each other and emotionally disengage. The *legal divorce* immerses them in the legal world of attorneys and courts because of dissolving a legal entity. The *economic divorce* involves the disbanding of the "small business" that any household is, usually with not enough financial resources to go around for both spouses, especially the former wife. The *co-parental divorce* involves arrangements for the custody and visitation of children.

The last two elements of any divorce are more subtle but nonetheless important. The *community divorce* involves all the family members and friends that have surrounded the couple; they are now faced with either choosing sides or deciding whether they can stay in contact with and help support both former spouses. And, finally, the *psychic divorce* involves each person regaining a sense of self apart from having been someone else's husband or wife.

As these "deaths" are swirling around a couple during a divorce, the rising and new life may seem far away indeed, but it will eventually come. Friends and family can only look on, try to be available, and pray for healing all around. (A subsequent remarriage would also go through each of these aspects in another transition to a new reality and a new life.)

A DAILY EXPERIENCE?

Dying and rising to new life can be seen readily in major life transitions, even in experiences as hard as divorce, but as we take a closer look at our experiences, we can also see it every day in small ways that may help us to understand more about the Paschal Mystery as a whole.

Going to sleep and waking, for example, is a clear example of dying and rising each day, dying to what the day now ending has brought, only to rise to the promise of a new day. (Someone recently suggested a prayer of gratitude and welcome as you open the drapes or shades on a new day, a lovely spiritual practice.) A bath or shower is also dying to the way your body had been and rising to a newer, cleaner you. Any kind of cleaning actually involves dying to the mess that was there—and sometimes temporarily creating a bigger one—to rise to a new kind of order and cleanliness. We could even say that any kind of learning is a process of dying to what we thought we knew to rise to new information and insights.

The list could go on of ways in which we die and rise in little ways every day, participating in the Paschal Mystery. The Jesuit theologian Fr. Karl Rahner, called this experience "dying in installments." What can we learn from this ever-present dynamic? Whether it's a major life transition, a good night's sleep, or a new way of getting to a favorite destination, we know that the new possibility has already begun in the midst of the "dying" involved in any of these experiences. With the eyes of faith, we can see that all this is part of the dying and rising of Christ again and again in our world today.

IN OUR MARRIAGES

In the book on marital spirituality mentioned earlier, *Marital Intimacy: A Catholic Perspective,* (now out of print), authors Joan Anzia and Mary Durkin look at four key movements in the course of a couple's intimacy that sheds light on the Paschal Mystery in the dynamics of a marriage. They describe the four movements of marital intimacy as Falling in Love,

Settling Down, Bottoming Out and Beginning Again, and they suggest that these stages happen at least once in every marriage and usually over and over again.

After a couple's Falling in Love and experiencing the powerful sense of grace in each other, they inevitably Settle Down, the authors say, to the dailiness in their relationship and the differences between them. But at some point, couples will come to the point of Bottoming Out. The little irritations that may have been overlooked now become too frustrating to ignore. The experience of conflict between them is not pleasant, and they may try to avoid it by blaming the other or even denying that a problem exists.

Whether they have been open about their times of conflict or not, Anzia and Durkin suggest that a couple finds themselves frightened in the midst of this conflict because they are at the foot of the cross. And, they say, the couple has an important choice to make. They may decide to settle for what they call a holding pattern, a false harmony and a twilight area where they don't really address the issue at hand. Or they may be willing to face the proverbial elephant in the room.

Paradoxically, it may take a major life transition to bring it to the surface. Anzia and Durkin wrote that a state of incomplete bottoming out can persist for years, until an event such as the leaving of the youngest child, a midlife career crisis, or a heart attack triggers an explosion so devastating that the marriage ends in divorce or goes into therapy with years of rage and resentment that must be faced and resolved.

If, instead of denying the problem, a couple is willing to face it and each other, each spouse needs to face his or her part in the hurt they've caused and ask for forgiveness. Then, and only then, can spouses really Begin Again to experience an even deeper love for each other. The couple must drop their defenses and trust that, even after their negative behaviors they are lovable persons who are important to each other. Though this seems unbelievable to us, it is true. When we are able to trust, we begin to understand, as Fr. Karl Rahner says, the profound depths of God's love. We can do this in our marriage when we trust the love with which our spouse forgives us.

Anzia and Durkin suggest that then the couple finds themselves Falling in Love again, but in a different and deeper way than when they were at that stage before. And so the cycle of marital intimacy goes, the authors suggest, which is both about the couple and their own growth together and also about the Paschal Mystery of the dying and rising of Christ in our midst.

DEATH OF A SPOUSE

When a couple vows to love each other till death, they can't begin to imagine that eventual day when their marriage will end upon the death of one of them. As their lives are more and more entwined, it's hard to envision a time when the other won't be there. Friends who have lost a spouse tell me that they never fully get over the loss and yet they can also feel closer to the spouse than ever. (On the other hand, we also hear of spouses who die in close proximity to each other, perhaps not wanting to be apart from the other for long.)

Whether the death of a spouse is sudden or lingering, it can be a time for the surviving spouse to take a look back at what they have experienced together and all the ways they have shared the grace, vocation, community, asceticism, incarnation, discernment and dying and rising through a life together that was far more than either of them could have imagined. There can often be mixed feelings at the spouse's passing. The process of grieving will be as different as each person is, and it is key to give that process all the time it needs. This allows the new life of memories and connections to emerge in the midst of remembering because, wonder of wonders, there is something of a birth involved with even something as seemingly final as death.

In her dazzling book *Radical Amazement: Contemplative Lessons From Black Holes, Supernovas, and Other Wonders of the Universe*, author Judy Cannato says that life and death are one mystery. That is what the Paschal Mystery teaches us. Death is unavoidable—but so is resurrection. We can be sure that dyings will disrupt our lives, and we may have some choice about how we respond. We can be alert to the arrival of resurrections, too, the surprising ways that new life fills our lives even in when death is happening. For we have the power to transcend, we can allow death to never have the final say."

❖ ❖ ❖

Debbie and Peter will be working on the "new normal" in their lives now that the kids are gone from the house, but this is far from the end of the process of dying and rising, of separation, marginality and re-integration in their lives. Just as Dietrich Bonhoeffer and Oscar Romero faced a death that led to a kind of new life they could embrace in faith, the dying and rising will continue. As long as we live we are part of the Mystical Body of Christ, and that means being part of the Paschal Mystery as well, with new life beginning in the midst of what can seem like loss and death.

FOR YOUR REFLECTION:

(After considering these questions individually I encourage you to talk, as a couple, about some or all of them.)

- For me, one of the strongest experiences of dying and rising in our marriage is _____.

- It was especially hard for me to go through _____ with you, but now I can see that it was the source of new life.

- Were there any hard times that threatened to pull us apart rather than bring us together? What were they?

- If we have children, how have their challenges and choices been a stress on us as a couple? How well did we support each other through those times?

- One of the dyings and risings that I wish we could have prevented someone we love from going through is _____.

- A kind of daily dying and rising that especially strikes me is _____.

- What choices and challenges lie ahead for us in the near future? What about beyond the more immediate issues? What strengths do we have to address our future together? What skills might we need to strengthen as we imagine our future?

Listening to Scripture

Jesus talking about the Paschal Mystery in our lives,
from the gospel of John (12:24–25):

Amen, amen, I say to you, unless a grain of wheat falls to the ground and dies, it remains just a grain of wheat; but if it dies, it produces much fruit. Whoever loves his life loses it, and whoever hates his life in this world will preserve it for eternal life.

FOR FURTHER EXPLORATION

Bridges, William, *Transitions: Making Sense of Life's Changes*. Addison-Wesley, 1980. A contemporary classic on the steps we experience during changes in our lives.

Cannato, Judy, *Radical Amazement: Contemplative Lessons From Black Holes, Supernovas, And Other Wonders of the Universe*. Sorin Books, 2006. A beautiful connection between what we now know about the universe and our own spirituality.

Cannato, Judy, *Field of Compassion: How the New Cosmology is Transforming Spiritual Life*. Sorin Books, 2010. More reflection on the spiritual implications of our universe and its dynamics.

Kidd, Sue Monk, *When The Heart Waits: Spiritual Direction for Life's Sacred Questions*. HarperSanFrancisco, 1990. The author's account of her own personal pain and awakening to God's grace.

Kubler-Ross, Elizabeth, *On Death and Dying: What the Dying Have to Teach Doctors, Nurses, Clergy and Their Own Families*. Scribner, 1969. An important early work in how to deal with death and the stages of grief.

Rohr, Richard. *Falling Upward: A Spirituality for the Two Halves of Life*. Jossey-Bass, 2011. Father Rohr, founder of the Center for Action and Contemplation, helps us to see how we grow spiritually more by our mistakes and problems than by our successes.

A Final Reflection

WE HAVE SEEN SOME of the ways that the facets of the spiritual life of grace, vocation, community, asceticism, incarnation, discernment, and dying and rising take shape in the life of couples. These components are, of course, interwoven with each other and always changing and growing. Each couple will live each of these aspects uniquely, but all these elements are there in each couple.

Spirituality, as we have seen, is not an abstract concept but something woven into the everyday reality of marriage in ways that are easy to miss if we aren't looking carefully for them. Hopefully, this opportunity to explore and reflect on your marriage in light of these components will give you a deeper awareness of your own marital spirituality and how to help it to continue to thrive.

> For this reason I kneel before the Father, from whom every family in heaven and on earth is named, that he may grant you in accord with the riches of his glory to be strengthened with power through his Spirit in the inner self, and that Christ may dwell in your hearts through faith; that you, rooted and grounded in love, may have strength to comprehend with all the holy ones what is the breadth and length and height and depth, and to know the love of Christ that surpasses knowledge, so that you may be filled with all the fullness of God.
>
> Now to him who is able to accomplish far more than all we ask or imagine, by the power at work within us, to him be glory in the church and in Christ Jesus to all generations, forever and ever. Amen.
>
> —Ephesians 3:14–21

Appendix: Applying This To the Finleys

THIS IS WHAT I wrote to my husband Mitch on the occasion of our fortieth wedding anniversary, and it can serve as one example of applying to a particular couple the aspects of marital spirituality that I discussed earlier. Here it is:

Dear Mitch,

Where do I begin? How can it possibly be that forty years have flown by since we first discovered the wonder of each other and were moved to pledge the rest of our lives together?

When I was considering what to write at this time of my life and thought about our fortieth anniversary approaching, I knew I wanted to try to say "thank you" by reflecting on what these past years have been with you. To recapture some of the energy we had at the beginning, I decided to go back and look at the letters you wrote me in the months between when we met and when we married, when we lived an hour and a half away from each other. We would see each other on weekends, but during the week our nearly-daily letters were a lifeline for both of us.

I hadn't opened those letters in all these years, but when I did, I was deeply struck, not only by the energy of our love at that time but also by the way in which all the aspects that I wanted to reflect on about marriage were already there as seeds in our beginnings as a couple. So I will be quoting from those letters at times—not to embarrass you, I hope, but to show how the tone had been set for what lay ahead for us. The Spirit was already at work in a way that we both somehow knew but could not have named then because we hadn't had a chance to fully live it yet.

Here's the way you expressed what the process of our writing to each other meant to you in one of your last letters just before I moved back to Spokane:

> The fact of our having been separated by a few miles during this time has given us, I think, the unique advantage of knowing each other thru letters, and for me at least this has been good, because often in letters I can express an aspect of myself that simply can't come out in any other way. In addition, I will always treasure among my warmest memories the incredible delight of receiving and opening a letter from you during our "courtship."

Who knows how much of the evidence of this precious time has been lost for other couples in an age of cell phones and texting and such, where there is no lasting record of the experience of delighting in one another at the very beginning?

❖ ❖ ❖

Because both of us had a strong academic and personal formation in spirituality and religion, we saw our relationship with each other as connected to our relationship with God from the very beginning. At one point you commented about our letters after our spending weekends together:

> We have those indescribably good times together—our *experience*—then we step back and, though separated by distance, together reflect on our experience, think of what new meaning we takes on, and write to each other about it. Is this not the process of "writing scripture," of speaking "the word" to each other, of reflecting on the experience we have of being God's "good news" to us? A little bit of theology all our own?

Although I couldn't see it at the time, as I look back now, after many years of having worked with engaged couples, I now realize some ways in which we were rather unprepared for a life together. Neither of us had great models of what marriage could be, and neither had dated much at all. We both had excellent educations but no real solid career prospects or plans—perhaps because of our impractical majors. In addition, we had no money saved. I came with most of my student loan debt, although thankfully Uncle Sam had helped you in that department because of your four years in the navy. We were older than many couples—you 27 and me 25—but basically, we were fairly inexperienced in the ways of the larger world.

We did have plenty going for us, though, when it came to some key areas. Not only did we have an academic background in our faith but we also had a strong commitment to what we believed and could share that closely with each other. We both had confidence in who we were, in our own maturity and our ability to handle difficult situations, although that would be tested for any possible cracks by marriage and later by children. From the beginning we had an awareness that our relationship was something we felt drawn to—called to—by Something, by Someone greater than ourselves, a presence that would sustain us through whatever we would encounter in the future.

Forty years later, I wish I could say that we have it all figured out. Yet we do know a lot more in some ways—and in others we probably know less than we thought we did then. I hope I haven't shared more here than you would be comfortable with, since I am the more extroverted of the two of us. I see the specifics of our lives as the way I think the Spirit has spoken in our midst, usually in a very hidden, sacred way.

After I reflect on the categories of grace, vocation, community, asceticism, incarnation, discernment, and dying and rising, I'll also explore where our life together may be headed from here as we walk further into the process of just being the two of us again, aging together and heading finally toward death.

I've probably told others more often than I've told you that I really don't know how you've put up with me for all these years, but the wonder of it is that you have. Thank you more than I can ever say for your amazingly constant and patient love through so many years. I do love you more each day—and, yes, I know that you would add that you love me more!

GRACE

The very fact of our meeting at all, I suppose, was an experience of grace. Neither of us were looking to meet someone to share our lives with—at least I know I wasn't.

Working in religious education at the parish in Pullman, I had come to a meeting of parish coordinators in Spokane in late August as the program year was beginning. Although I'd even been told by a professor in grad school in religious education at Fordham that I'd never meet my future spouse in religious education, at the meeting there was this interesting guy, who seemed a bit befuddled and who was trying to look like he knew what he was doing. You had recently graduated from Santa Clara University in religious studies and didn't really know much about working in religious education, it seemed.

I still have a vague recollection of noticing that you might have needed some wardrobe help; maybe there were plaids and stripes somehow besides the corduroy jacket that I think you were wearing. But Something began that day between us, the beginnings of the experience of grace.

How was our meeting and relationship an experience of grace, of the energy of God? If God is love, as the epistle of John tells us, then we were both flooded with an experience of God, seemingly out of the blue and in the midst of not expecting it.

Many would say, "Well, that was just good old falling in love—nothing more." But for us that amazing experience quickly took on spiritual overtones. I'll let you explain it: "I feel like maybe for the first time in my life—or at least in a completely new way—I know something of what 'God' means, what 'God' is all about. And all because of *you*. Because of *us*."

And again, in your own inimitable style:

> Whenever I think of you or think of you thinking of me—*me!* of all people—I rather quietly go bananas. A joy far beyond mere "whoopee," far deeper and more silent.

This experience of grace quickly becomes an experience where ordinary language doesn't quite hold what we're trying to say, and we resort to music or poetry. In the same letter quoted above, you shared lines from a couple of lovely poems by Mark Van Doren, a favorite poet of yours, including:

> Oh, but I wonder,
> Oh, but I know,
> Who comforts like raisins,
> Who kisses like snow.
> —Mark Van Doren, *Dunce Songs*, #6

The love we experienced was always rooted in God for both of us. It was an energy that began almost immediately to give us each a fuller sense of ourselves, allowing us to grow in ways that were different than if we each had been on our own. The power of it was pretty mind-boggling, perhaps especially because to that point neither of us had experienced a serious love relationship in our lives, apart from an early romantic crush. You talked about it this way:

> How, I sometimes wonder, can I bear so much love; yet I do and I am so filled with a deep and intense happiness that I think sometimes I'll burst! . . . Each evening when I light our candle at supper time, suddenly I am filled with a deep calm and I could pray on and on, prayers of praise and thanksgiving, of petition for courage and fidelity; of you and I and deep into the center of my soul, begging for love to give to you, all of it, all of me. My love, my life, how I want only to be with you.

Already we were becoming a "sacrament" for each other, not in the official sense of what we would receive at our wedding, but in the everyday sense of being a visible, tangible sign of God's invisible, intangible love for us. There was a joy much deeper than words can hold, one that will pop up even now when we least expect it. We can see it in the way other couples are with each other at times, as well. I can remember sensing more energy in everything around me in those days. This was the beginning for us of a deeper sacramental imagination, one that can see God at work everywhere, once you begin to look for it.

❖ ❖ ❖

This is probably as good a place as any to share a reading that you had found that described some of what we had already experienced, although not as ideally or as churchy as this can sound. It was the second reading from our wedding—more about that later—that I found carefully typed out in the box with your letters. It's from a letter of Tertullian, an early third century Christian author, to his wife:

> How beautiful, then, the marriage of two Christians, who are one in hope, one in desire, one in the way of life they follow, both servants of the same Master. Nothing divides them, either in flesh or in spirit. They are in very truth, two in one flesh; and where there is but one flesh there is also but one spirit. They pray together, they worship together, they fast together; instructing one another, encouraging one another, strengthening one another. Side by side they face difficulties and persecution, share their consolations. They have no secrets from one another, they never shun each other's company; they never bring sorrow to each other's hearts. . . Hearing and seeing this, Christ rejoices. To such as these he gives his peace.

❖ ❖ ❖

I think that often we're only able to sense God's presence when we look back –like this reflection, I guess—and see how God was at work, not only in some key experiences but also in the daily ones where we took that Presence for granted. When we *remember*, we recall *again (re)* that we are *members* of one another and that God is part of that reality, not as an outside force, but in our case as the energy between us, drawing us together with a breathtaking force.

And this force, this grace, hits at times when we least expect it. In the middle of a letter talking about something else, you suddenly inserted this way of celebrating that wonder-filled energy: "Hey!! *I love you*! (Fireworks, sparklers, great display of colorful wonders in God's heavens.)"

VOCATION

Our life journeys to the point of meeting one another had already led us in some pretty interesting directions. After high school I had entered a Franciscan novitiate in Portland, Oregon, having turned down a full honors scholarship to Gonzaga University, but then returned to the campus for the Spring semester after finding that religious life—at least in that community—was not where I felt called. After finishing at Gonzaga I spent one year in grad school in Religious Education at Chicago Theological Seminary, adjacent to the University of Chicago, and the following year I finished the same Master's degree at Fordham University in the Bronx. I'd also had a couple of opportunities to go to Europe, mainly France and a few other countries, because of a connection with the Taizé community, an ecumenical monastic community located in rural Burgundy. That community had, and has, an amazingly deep spirituality that drew me and many young people from throughout the world to reflect and pray together there. Eventually I ended up back in Spokane working at a couple jobs, one of which was directing religious education in Pullman, Washington, home of Washington State University in the middle of the lovely Palouse wheat fields.

Meanwhile, you had entered the Navy after graduating from high school in Walla Walla and ended up seeing some interesting places yourself, including Beeville, Texas, Norfolk, Virginia, and a couple of locations on the island of Oahu in Hawaii. You never really got to do what you had signed up for, which was being a photographer's mate; you had enjoyed photography as a hobby and a summer job when you were in high school. Instead, the U.S. Navy ended up training you to maintain aircraft logs and records—I hope I have the terminology right! Although you thought you didn't have the grades or academic ability to go to college, you started reading seriously while in the Navy—a lot of literary classics and books about the spiritual life, including Thomas Merton's *The Seven Storey Mountain*.

As a result of your reading and a long-time desire, upon finishing four years in the Navy you entered the Holy Cross Brothers. In the process of formation with that community you also saw various parts of the country, ending up in Mountain View, California, staying with the Brothers there and attending Santa Clara University. (As accomplished and bright as you clearly are, it still surprises me that you were admitted to Santa Clara only on special presidential permission because of your grades from high school.)

Toward the end of your college experience, it became, I guess, increasingly clear that staying with the Brothers was not where you were feeling called, and so you left Holy Cross and finished your degree at Santa Clara as a layperson. Soon thereafter you sought and found a job in the Spokane area, which is what led to our meeting.

Who knows whether or how we would have met, had our life histories been even a little different. Through the years working with engaged couples I have heard amazing stories about how couples met, including what can look like repeated attempts on God's part to finally bring a couple together.

❖ ❖ ❖

So, both of us had experienced opportunities to travel and study and now were back in Spokane, where we both had roots. We had each experienced a number of good places that were not where we belonged. What helped us recognize that we were right for each other when we met? I'm not sure that either of us could fully answer that question even now. We didn't have the experience I've heard of at times of seeing each other across a room and knowing "that's the person I'm going to marry."

After our first meeting, I knew I wanted to spend more time with you, so when the opportunity for a professional workshop in Seattle came up that you were planning to attend in late September, I definitely signed up. We were part of a small group of religious education directors from Spokane and mainly did some sightseeing together. But I remember trying to subtly (or not so subtly, perhaps) make myself apparent to you—changing tables in the hotel meeting room, for example, so that I could sit closer to you. And when we went on an underground tour of the streets and settings under the current streets of Seattle, I even acted a bit frightened so that you would stay close, which is not usually like me.

The rest of the time in Seattle was special, riding the ferry and going out to dinner—always with the group—before we left to go home, me to Pullman, you to Spokane. I think we both knew something important—perhaps life-changing—had happened, but neither of us knew how to talk about it, either with each other or with anyone else. I drove up to Spokane the next weekend and called you, asking if you would show me the new church at the parish where you worked—I was shameless. I almost didn't catch that you said, "Kathy who?" when I called. Later you told me that was because you couldn't believe that it was really me on the phone!

The reason you were so surprised to hear my voice is that you had written a letter to me, which I hadn't yet received, awaiting me when I returned to Pullman in the event you didn't explain how you felt while I was in town! As it ended up, you showed me the church, we went and sat by the river, and gradually told each other how we felt; you even came over to my parents' house to meet them later that day.

Thankfully, I still have that letter, a glimpse into what had been going on in you as you were beginning to experience this sense of vocation, of a call to be with me:

> For better or "worser" I am rarely at a loss for words—but the time spent in your company in Seattle leaves me pretty much that way. . .. being with you has affected me deeply in a way new to my experience. I am, in a way I do not understand, simply overwhelmed by the goodness and the love that you are. The fact that we have known each other for so brief a time makes this all the more a mystery—something of a source of confusion—to me. I find myself wanting very much simply to be with you.

❖ ❖ ❖

So, here we were, both having searched in the past for other ways to live our faith and our lives, embracing possibility and an amazing amount of energy where we least expected it: in a relationship with each other. We both knew that a vocation was not some message from God written on the clouds—or even delivered by someone wise. Because we had tried other possibilities and commitments with our lives, we had a sense that it might be there when we least expected it, even when we were making other plans. (I had actually been taking Spanish at Washington State University recently, with vague plans to go work in the Church in Latin America.)

Our relationship developed further as the days and weeks went by, and at Thanksgiving we were ready to announce our engagement, although we've never really been able to retrace exactly how we came to that decision. From the outside, the timeline of our relationship may look like a whirlwind, getting married by early March, but I don't remember experiencing it that way.

There was both a calm, unfolding feeling and also an amazing amount of energy, as paradoxical as that sounds. I am convinced that the Holy Spirit is the source of that kind of energy, an energy that the first disciples experienced in wind and flames—and the kind we might experience today as the electricity that powers much of what surrounds us. You even talked about the power we were experiencing: "Life is becoming something else again. Deeply, mysteriously, quietly—yet with the forceful inevitability of the power which creates the universe."

❖ ❖ ❖

But what shape was this vocation, this relationship going to take? Our unique vocation certainly took time to unfold. During the first few months of our marriage you were working as a bank messenger, and I was commuting to Pullman two days a week to try to accomplish most of the work I had previously been doing in a full week in the parish there. But then came word that you had been accepted for graduate work in theology at Marquette University in Milwaukee, a place neither of us had ever been, and so we set out for the Midwest. Once we got there I found a job in a parish once more doing religious education work, a strand of the story I'll pick up later.

❖ ❖ ❖

Even more important than what we were *doing* was trying to understand who we were called to *be*, which was already something you were considering in your letters. You wrote:

> I have, without really being able to restrain myself, been talking to the teachers I've been "home visiting" this week about marriage, and the more I listen to what they have to say the more I am convinced of the unique character of our love, and of the goodness of marriage and of how good it would be for us and for those we would serve . . . and for the Christian community as a whole. The thought of us going at and living life each day together is such an intensely joyous and quiet and moving thought!

When I think about some of the specific qualities of our vocation as a couple, besides *service*, mentioned in your letter above, I also see the importance of what I would call *practical spirituality*, helping us and others to link our faith with our everyday experience and reality. Underlying it all has been *prayer*, helping us to listen to where we were being called, and the value of *simplicity* in our life together. I'll talk more about the specific *decisions* shaped by each of these qualities when I talk about discernment later, but I want to say something more about each of these elements in our vocation together.

Exactly how were we to be of service to others? Before long in our marriage we ended up preparing engaged couples for marriage for many years, work that I continue to do even now. And you were already writing and even had a job doing some editorial work during your graduate studies, while I was always interested in teaching and had taught at least one summer class at Gonzaga before we met.

Those early experiences bore fruit, I guess. Besides numerous articles, you have ended up writing over 30 books, and during my teaching at Gonzaga for many years I've written eight so far. In addition, we've been educators together and separately via speaking engagements and workshops.

Whenever one or the other of us would take a job that seemed more responsible financially, one that was usually not connected to working with marriage and family and practical spirituality topics—what we took to calling "a real job" at our house—it seemed like we kept being called back to what we both have ended up doing, which is reflecting on our lives. Our experience illustrates my definition of a vocation or ministry: *what you can't not be doing*—not great grammar, but I think it summarizes what we've been called to do and be.

Whether in writing or in teaching, then, the shape of our lives has ended up to be the raw material for much of what we have reflected on—in a more literal way, perhaps, than may be the case for many other couples. This has helped shape, I think, our sense of practical spirituality, of trying to understand and articulate the ways our faith experience intersects with the daily realities of grocery shopping and meals and laundry and such. Most of the time, of course, we haven't been aware of life's holiness; just as in all the aspects of our vocation I'm trying to describe here, we have certainly made mistakes and not been aware of them until we looked back—if then— which, of course, made the importance of prayer all the greater.

We knew from the beginning that prayer needed to be a part of what we were about. Besides our own daily prayer and trying to listen for God's voice and energy, together we planned a half-day of prayer with a priest friend a few days before the wedding. And the night before our wedding we also invited our friends and family to join us for a prayer vigil at a small local chapel. It created a comfortable way for people to connect with us as they came into town for the wedding. I remember that you had collected a number of favorite prayers and readings for people to reflect on if they wanted to during that time.

We have both made prayer a priority in our lives, but each in our own way. You have gone on retreat, for example, to the nearest Trappist monastery a number of times, which is how I started going there, and now I have gone there annually for many years. I try to take one day a month as a quiet prayer day, often at the House of Prayer just north of town, while you pray in other daily ways. Although we have tried to find other ways of praying together besides meal prayers, nothing has ever felt right for us. But I tell couples that I work with that I don't think that makes us any less holy as a couple than other couples that do pray together daily; we're just different and continue to explore what works uniquely for us.

We both had an interest in trying to live with fewer possessions than many people thought were necessary when we met, but we also had to work out the specifics of that. We even tried not having a newspaper or telephone when we were first married, but that didn't last for long. Though both of us admired the radical simplicity of the Catholic Worker movement, started by Dorothy Day and based on hospitality for the poor and even antiwar activism, but this also didn't seem to be where we were called. The career choices we *did* feel called to translated to income levels that would never be particularly affluent, so in some ways the simplicity issue sort of took care of itself. I do remember having crates and trunks for tables in our living room and plenty of second-hand furniture for many years and being quite comfortable with what we had. And I'm still glad that we put off owning a television for many years.

Our vocation as a couple seems to have had these characteristics of service, practical spirituality, prayer and simplicity; other couples we know have other unique combinations of qualities and traits that make their marriage what it is and who they are.

❖ ❖ ❖

Looking back now, our vocation has clearly unrolled through the years. Although the theme of our wedding was "Here begins a new life" and inscribed on our rings is "And the two" (on yours) and "shall become one" (on mine), we didn't have much of a clue of what we were stepping into and what was to come. I'll return to the process of our unfolding more later, but wanted to end this section about vocation by sharing our version of the prayer of Charles de Foucauld, a wonderful Christian figure of the late 19th and early 20th century. His prayer was for an individual; we changed it for us as a couple, and we said it together at our wedding just before the final blessing:

> Father,
> We abandon ourselves into your hands;
> do with us what you will.
> Whatever you may do, we thank you;
> We are ready for all, we accept all.
> Let only your will be done in us,
> and in all your creatures—
> We wish no more than this, O Lord.
> Into your hands we commend our life;
> for we love you, Lord, and so need to give ourselves,
> [and with boundless confidence,]
> to surrender ourselves into your hands without reserve.
> for you are our Father.

When I looked up this prayer, I found the phrase here in brackets, which I really like.

COMMUNITY

Through the years we have always been blessed with an amazing community of friends and family who have sustained us in many ways, although like many couples, I think we just assumed that this support would always be there and didn't see how truly precious it was.

Our first awareness was that the two of us were quickly becoming a "community" of love for each other, and there was for us a kind of "trinity" to our love, a taste of the community of love we see in God.

You mentioned this in one of your letters: "It seems that whenever I pray now it is for 'us' more than for 'me.' It's just so natural to do so, it simply comes out that way. I am no longer I, but I can only think and pray as us."

Many engaged couples with whom I work are certainly aware of the dynamic of love encircling the two of them, but often that's all they're aware of. They don't usually think about the parents, siblings and friends surrounding them, people who have helped make them who they are to this point in their lives and who now are watching them enlarge and deepen their love energies as they incorporate this new key person into their lives. Likely because we had met in the context of a group of support, the importance of these others in our lives had already been clear.

❖ ❖ ❖

Our connection with others was also evident at the beginning of our wedding. Just after the entrance song at the Student Chapel at Gonzaga the guests saw slides of both of us throughout our lives, from infancy up to that present moment together. The music group was singing during these images "See these two before you, Lord, you who gave them life. . .."—a slight modification of a Song of Baptism that said, "See this child before you, Lord, you who gave him/her life. . .."

Captured in the photographs were many of the people attending the wedding, people whose lives had been intimately woven with ours. In a very real sense it was because of them that we were now who we were and not someone else. In fact, in his homily Fr. Tom Royce, who presided at our wedding, alluded to this very idea by mentioning, "There are many people who have been God's love for the two of you in your lives; now you are to be the main shape of that love for one another."

I tell my marriage students and engaged couples that a married couple is a sign of God's love to each other, to the others around them, and because of others' love in their lives. Two of these dimensions involve *others*; we don't do this love-thing on our own.

Mitch, you also talked about how we were becoming a sign to others in one of your letters in a part addressed to God:

> Father of we two who have been given to one another by your love, above all we thank you for such goodness. Keep us faithful to you, lead us into the life together that you will for us. Increase our love for one another till you alone are present to those around us. Bring us to the way where we can do the most to bring others to you.

As with most couples, if we tried now to list all the people who have been a part of our lives, the list would be extensive, and the contexts would be many and varied. Many couples relocate, as we did early, widening our circle. Friends from work and hobbies, as well as people we got to know through our kids' schools and activities, and those from many other contexts have continued to uniquely stretch our lives and our awareness.

❖ ❖ ❖

One of the most supportive communities for us has been a particular group of couples and families who have been there for us in many ways through the years and continuing to sustain us even now. We met these couples through shared service; all of us were helping work with engaged couples through the diocesan Marriage Preparation Weekends,. Most of the helping couples had babies already or had babies on the way—now young adults in their thirties, most of them married themselves! Even though we lived in various neighborhoods and parishes around town, pretty early on we started meeting monthly to pray together for families and engaged couples and to socialize, sharing many an evening focusing on joys and sorrows, celebrating a birthday or two (complete with "groaner" birthday cards) and often a meal together.

Along the way, we created a babysitting co-op when the kids were younger, including a complex system of points for how many kids and how many hours we watched each others' children. Today I wonder why we kept such careful track of those points, because I think we all knew it would never come out even, but that didn't matter. We organized picnics and kids' birthday celebrations, and years later we followed up with memorable send-offs when gathering to honor the young people among us graduating from high school. After showing slides of the graduates through the years, a lit candle then made the rounds of the group, and recollections and good wishes were offered as these young people headed off into their respective futures. And, even more recently, there have been plenty of weddings and parties and baby showers, as their lives and ours continued to expand.

In our mobile society some couples have had to leave our group for various reasons, but when you and I considered the possibility of relocating at one point, we realized that it would have been nearly as hard to leave our couples group as it would be to leave our own families.

Supports like these are key for a marriage. In fact, my primary wish for the future of the engaged couples with whom I work would be for them to discover some couples with healthy marriages—ones where honest communication and deep affection and respect seem evident—with whom they can develop a community of support for one another.

❖ ❖ ❖

Although our own experience of community with people living in other countries and cultures is not as strong as some couples we know, our circle of awareness and concern has been expanded somewhat beyond our own cultural and national borders. We have been involved with a group called Family to Family, an organization that pairs families in this area with families in rural, poor Guatemala, where the Spokane diocese has a mission and a self-help program to improve the living conditions for the people there. Families only stay on the program for two or three years so as not to make them dependent on the money which is contributed. At one point we had an opportunity to go see some of these families in Guatemala so that you could write about the organization.

Through the years we have had a picture on the refrigerator of the current Guatemalan family that we are helping. It has helped us—and our kids when they were home—begin to imagine what life is like in a very different living situation, such as living with dirt floors and often without running water. The opportunity to widen our circle of concern and connection beyond our own borders in an increasingly global society was a gift to all of us.

In our personal culture, the two of us don't always deal with the people around our marriage in the same ways, which I see largely as a function of our gender and introversion/extroversion differences. For example, you're almost always the one who wants to go home from a gathering first and who would rather stay in one location when we vacation rather than move around to various places, as I would prefer. I find that there's almost always some amount of difference between introverts and extroverts in any marriage, and in navigating these it can be tough to articulate one's preferences and needs and hard to accommodate them. Thankfully, none of these differences are major ones for us; on the one hand, it would be boring being married to a clone, and yet when there are extreme differences in a marriage, they can present some significant challenges to a couple.

❖ ❖ ❖

In recent years we've both found our own individual communities of support, as well as the shared community that sustains our marriage. Years ago, surrounded by with three sons, you and even a male cat, I found I needed to seek out some feminine energy in my life. I have been a part of a women's spirituality group that has met monthly for many years. You were part of a writers' group many years ago, and in recent years you've connected with the local bluegrass music association, a group of folks all interested in playing and supporting bluegrass music in this area. Having individual interests and supports strengthens our marriage instead of weakening it. Although the challenges have looked different at various times in our marriage, we need to keep striking a balance between being overly involved in each other's lives—enmeshed—and being too separated from each other.

We have certainly been embarrassingly rich in friends and people who have been gifts in our lives, as we reflect on them now. We'll never be able to adequately thank all of them, but we can continue to hold them in our hearts with gratitude and try to be for them the faithful love and support that they have been for us.

ASCETICISM

The word "asceticism" sounds grim indeed, with echoes of religious self-denial, austerity and harsh discipline, either imposed or chosen. But as couples we make daily choices that need to take into account the other person and the priority of that relationship in our lives, even though we may have never thought about those choices as asceticism. Although we're not as disparate as some couples we know, there are still plenty of differences in our temperaments, some of which were evident to us even when we were going together. Here is what I wrote in an early letter:

> Mitch, you are far more aware of time and focused on being somewhere early than I am. You would say I'm chronically late, while I would say that I'm more relaxed about time than you are. (That has actually gotten much better with the years, although it

can still be a tension at times.) I'm a bit more of a night person than you are, while you would rather head to bed earlier and rise earlier than I would *and* you can fall asleep right away—luckily, that's not an extreme difference between us. We're pretty similar when it comes to planning vs. spontaneity, but I have seen that be a real problem with some couples with whom I have worked. We have both been known to be a bit stubborn, and often it's only after we've been shown to be wrong in our ideas—usually many more times than one—that we will concede that we may have been mistaken.

There are plenty of other personal differences that have been challenges at times for us to work with, such as the degree of cleanliness and clutter each of us is comfortable with. I won't say which of the two of us is neater, but a glance at each of our computer desks would quickly disclose the answer! And as the more extroverted of the two of us, I tend to want to talk about issues a bit more than you do, and I like getting together with others more often than you. Yet another frequent area where choosing the good of the other over one's own preferences comes into play is the question of when to choose to communicate with the other, especially when you'd rather not just then. Both of us have had at least a few times when it would have been easier to nurse hurt feelings than to let the other person know what he or she did or said that hurt more than the other knew.

In one of your letters you mentioned, "I wish I could begin to tell you how beautiful it is that you *don't* feel constrained in any way to be anything but yourself with me." And you went on to say that you didn't like it when women play dumb and have a "cute/giggly routine." But I don't think you fully realized until years later that you ended up with a person who may speak her mind more often than you might like!

When it comes to cleaning, we each have the places that we notice as not being tidy enough more often than the other person would, such as the stove or the bathroom, making the bed or even the top of the refrigerator. Generally, I find that I tend to be more focused on household details, which is generally true with women, but that isn't always the case in our day-to-day experience. What is true is that all these very little irritations can build up and are ways in which we need to "die a little" each day to be able to manage with another who doesn't do things the way we do them—which is the right way, of course!

Beside the irritations and differences between us, there are also the ways that asceticism comes into play as a couple, especially as we work together and take time for us as a couple.

We only worked together in the same office setting a couple of times, but that had its own challenges and gave me an added appreciation for couples who have worked together for many years. When we share a speaking engagement, the challenges are clearly evident. Not only do you focus more on giving specific information while I tend to want to build in as much process and participation as possible, you also would rather "wing it" when you get up to talk, while I want to plan it out ahead of time. (The problem with either of us being spontaneous at the moment is that we have given presentations together so often that we end up saying what the other has carefully planned to say.) At any rate, while sharing the podium together is enjoyable, it is also a significant challenge for us—and likely so for other couples.

Another way asceticism takes place in our marriage is making time for us as a couple. We know many couples who plan a regular date night as we do, and I always recommend it to engaged couples.

I can still recall when you informed me within the first weeks after our oldest was born that we would be going out for a date night. I protested that he was too little to be left with a sitter, but you assured me that he would be just fine, and of course, he was. And that began many years of weekly date nights—occasionally interrupted by sick kids or births or major illnesses, but overall quite a regular practice of ours. To follow through on our commitment to a date night, plenty of background preparations were necessary like preparing dinner for our kids, writing reminders for the sitter, as well as picking him or her up. Even now, we still have our weekly date night, long after our kids are gone from our house.

It may seem strange to talk about going out for dinner and a movie—which has been the usual shape of our outings—as a discipline, but there have been a number of times when it would have been easier to just stay home—and often collapse—after the kids had gone to bed. But I was always glad that we took the time to be with each other, even if we were so tired that nothing significant ever got said.

❖ ❖ ❖

Another element that has "paid off" for us, I think, that is paradoxical is *time alone* for each of us. Experiences in solitude and our individual hobbies have helped sustain us as a couple by nourishing us each individually. Whether that was the nightly walks you would take once the kids were in bed when they were tiny or the monthly prayer days that I started taking when they were older or our separate activities—reading or biking, your banjo playing or my knitting or sewing—it's been important that we both know what can sustain us so that we have more energy to give to the both of us.

As important as time to ourselves and with other friends and even work and the kids are to us, one way that asceticism also takes place in marriage is fidelity to us as a couple. Thankfully, we've never had to deal with any emotional or sexual infidelity, but the asceticism of marriage includes making choices that keep each other in the center of our energies and our attention and also continuing to work on keeping our relationship alive and growing.

Little did we know forty years ago that all of the choices we would be making, even when they were about self-care, would need to take the other person into account. And the "martyrdom" we were being called to was a gentle, subtle one, an unselfishness that now has mostly become second nature but also one that still means setting aside what I want to do on a regular basis for what is better for the both of us.

INCARNATION

"And the Word was made flesh . . ." (John 1:14) That's in a sense what happened for us: the words "love" and "Mitch and Kathy" were made flesh in our lives together, in our relationship—and as Robert Frost would say, that has made all the difference. Although the word "incarnation" usually refers to Jesus as God made flesh, the reality of the holistic experience of our relationship is also very incarnational; the experience of falling in love with you brought a unity to who I was that I couldn't have imagined beforehand.

Here's how you put it in one letter: ". . . we are the greatest thing ever to happen to us—what a good thing God has done. As you said, indeed through each other God is recreating each of us."

And a little later on the same day, after talking about each of us feeling better about being a man and a woman in a new way, you said:

> O you gentle gift of grace to me, you event of life to me, you fine and loving girl and woman from God to me . . . you laughter and quiet softness of your breath to me .. You opening on the truth to me . . . I love you . . .

Rather suddenly and quite completely, there were connections for us in our lives where before there had been disconnects and voids—with each other and with ourselves. We had grown up in a culture where the soul and spirit were seen to be good but where sexuality and the body weren't considered quite right but rather topics to blush at and to be spoken of in hushed tones or giggled over—thanks largely to a dualistic idea of the human person that can be traced all the way back to the ancient Greeks. Thankfully, we now began to see ourselves and our relationship in a more whole and holy way.

After talking in one of the letters about being physically close and listening to one another's breathing, you said,

> And I am once again (more so than before) given concrete evidence of the truth that is God: always there, straining and groaning, seeking with an infinite desire, love begs to be born in our hearts.

This holistic awareness was also evident in our sexuality, but not only there. Neither of us had even dated much, so our sexuality was a new and powerful language for us to be able express our love for each other. I remember that there was an amazing lack of any embarrassment or awkwardness with each other because it quickly became clear that there was nothing to be afraid of in expressing our love for each other.

We did some reading and discussing about sexuality, which was very helpful for us, and I encourage engaged couples to do so, too. The book *The Joy of Sex* had fairly recently come out, and we giggled over some of the pictures within its pages. We also discovered a book that suggested that some cultures thought that chocolate was an aphrodisiac, and all I can remember of a poem that accompanied this thought was the final line, which was, ". . . cocoa coursing through their veins." Sexuality was a playful and helpful way for us to express the power of the love that seemed to grow as time went on.

We were called to be one, as you recalled in a letter:

> It says in Genesis 2:24 that "a man leaves his father and mother and clings to his wife, and that two of them become one body." I suppose there is a sexual reference here, but to me it seems much more inclusive—it is speaking of a way of being, of existing, as "one body." That is what we are called to become—we are to be "one body." And that is what I want with all my heart.

❖ ❖ ❖

Through the years our lovemaking has certainly changed as we have changed as a couple; for one thing, being too tired at times to make love now isn't related to the kids' needs. There have been challenges along the way because often when one of us is "in the mood," the other may not be. To say the least, it has been an important way for us to appreciate each other, to relax, to celebrate making up after forgiving, to play together, and to lose ourselves in each other. And we continue even now to learn what the other enjoys and doesn't appreciate.

This Being One and lovemaking eventually resulted in three little Finleys, and their presence certainly made the incarnational aspect even stronger because it seems that family life is often about wiping noses or bottoms. As an embodiment of our love, it was so amazing to watch them come into our world and our lives and to grow, discovering—and showing us—the wonders around them.

I've already mentioned how they helped us understand how to pray with our bodies more. Whether a holiday or any day, the kids helped us to appreciate the ways in which hugs and looking for bugs and a simple picnic on the grass were ways to see God at work around us. Though the "kids" have grown and gone now, that longing for wholeness and being fully connected continues. Here's how you expressed it all those years ago:

> I love you more deeply as the days go by, and all I pray for is more unity with the Spirit of truth which is God's gift to us in Christ. And strength and courage to love you more—to not fear the risks which real love demands. . .. I want so much to love you more and more in spirit and in truth, fully humanly, completely in God, personally and as you really are, spiritually, physically, psychologically, the totality that is *you*, in all ways. . . a goal I pray I may never abandon. It's a goal I guess I'll never fully attain, and at times I will fail (we both will), but with God's grace to keep me going, I will keep on trying. I love you with so deep a love.

DISCERNMENT

The process of our lives unfolding together obviously involved plenty of choices for us, and the pattern of those decisions is a helpful way to see the fabric of our lives taking shape.

We certainly haven't always made our choices all that reflectively and prayerfully—although we've tried to, especially at key points—and we haven't always made them well, in hindsight. But I'd like to explore some of our choices through the years and how they have shaped our lives and who we have grown to be; many of these decisions are much like those of other couples, while some are more unique to the two of us.

❖ ❖ ❖

Before we met, not only had each of us made a series of choices that had made us who we were, but then there also was the decision to marry each other—perhaps one that may have appeared a bit hasty from the outside, but we knew surprisingly quickly that we shared so many values in common and that this was where God was drawing each of us. The only time that I ever briefly doubted that decision was the day that you appeared on the doorstep of my apartment in Pullman in the middle of the week, which was a time when we never usually saw each other. You explained that you had been let go from your job, a job that I didn't even know was causing problems for you. It made me wonder briefly what else you hadn't told me, but after we agreed that we would tell each other everything, even the problems, we were fine from then on.

As I mentioned earlier, as newlyweds we decided to see if we could live differently than the accepted norms to try to simplify our lives. We didn't have a phone or a newspaper at first, but that didn't last too long. And apart from a brief time when we were given one, we decided not to have a television—a choice that became quite challenging once three little ones came along later. We didn't want to use our time, energy and imagination on values that we were told were important but which really didn't matter to us. We also needed to establish a joint financial account and a way of dealing with our money—certainly more sophisticated than the envelope marked "Bananas" in which you kept all your cash when I first met you!

We each had older cars—very used—when we met, and before long we decided to get rid of your old Chrysler, which we called the Green Machine, and just share the VW Bug that I had been driving. That worked fine until we decided to move to the Midwest four months later, and the poor vehicle threw a rod trying to pull all our earthly belongings in a four by six trailer over the mountains headed east!

The reason we were trekking there was for you to go to graduate school at Marquette University, which meant leaving behind almost everything we were familiar with but also knowing that graduate school made sense for you and was what you wanted to do. Not only was it an adventure for us as newlyweds, but it was to prove rich for us in ways we couldn't have imagined. I remember feeling a strong freedom to our lives at that point, some of which is still there, but much of that dynamic just goes with being newly married and on the brink of so many possibilities. Here's how you put it:

> Our love seems to be of such a texture that it could bear far more than we can imagine . . . Also, I continue to be impressed and staggered by the simple eyes-wide-open strength of your desire to be with me and share life, even in unimpressive circumstances.

It brings home to me again and again that all you really want is to be with *me*, not me-provided-there's-plenty-of-money-and-a-classy-place-to-live.

As we headed to Milwaukee and got established there, it gave us a chance to know who we were as a couple, apart from our families. We were very fortunate to be a part of an incredible parish in inner-city Milwaukee, one that drew from all over the city and also provided—and still does—a meal for those who need it six days a week, thanks to volunteers from all over the city and its suburbs. Not only were we involved with helping with that meal, usually one night a week, but we found an amazing community of friends through the parish who were intentional about how to live their lives and their faith. We were there in Milwaukee for two years, and after some challenges I'll say more about later, we returned west.

❖ ❖ ❖

We knew we both missed the Northwest, but we didn't find any jobs we wanted in Spokane, so we ended up for a year in Bremerton, across Puget Sound from Seattle, with a position for you at a parish that was still finding itself, which also turned into a part-time responsibility for me, while we got to know more good friends and enjoyed where we were living. It was especially fun because we could walk to the Seattle ferry and could spend the evening in Seattle and then take a later boat home.

The next year we were able to move back to Spokane because the diocese here wanted a married couple to head the Family Life Office, which had already been established and run by two different priests. In each of these moves, there was far more than logistics and packing and unpacking to consider. It was a question of where we would be most free to use the gifts we had been given and most able to grow closer to God and closer to each other.

After living in one more apartment when first returning to Spokane, we were able to move into our first house, a pretty simple one that had more room, room that we would need because our first child was on the way. Not only did we try to furnish and decorate the house simply—sort of early Goodwill—but I remember learning to cook a lot of dishes myself so that we would cut down on processed foods that we were eating and using. There were also opportunities for plenty of exercise in our lives; you would take evening walks, and I could walk or bike to the park and to Gonzaga when I was teaching and working there. We also used the library a lot, especially as the kids came along.

Our work in the Family Life Office gave us an opportunity to connect our changing lives with the way our Church was responding to those needs, so you worked on projects like a Marriage Preparation policy for the diocese, and we worked on a newsletter for families together. I also started realizing that what was happening to me and to us needed more prayer resources, so we helped organize several days of reflection for mothers of young children, as well as planning several pregnancy reflection groups to help make the connection between spirituality and family life clearer. We also had the privilege of being involved with several national meetings about family life topics.

You had begun writing on a part-time basis for various periodicals, and then that took on more shape as the jobs ended with the diocese, first for me and then for you.

❖ ❖ ❖

With three sons under four by the time we had been married less than seven years, life was busy at our house, to say the least. There had been so many choices to make about and for them: what I should eat and do during pregnancy, how to handle the birth itself and then whether to breast feed them, and gradually there were plenty of decisions about ordering their lives for safety and health, as well as their discipline. While things were certainly busy, there were certainly plenty of delights as they discovered the amazing world around them.

We tried to feed their imaginations as well as their bodies well, with no TV and plenty of music and stories, both recorded and in books, mainly from the library. We also tried to encourage their imaginations with the toys they had—and didn't have, like guns. The problem was that, being boys, they used their hands, sticks and even Legos instead! I loved what you would tell them when they complained of being bored in the summers. Rather than give them some suggestions of what they could do with their time, which was my first inclination, you counseled them to lay on the floor, look up at the ceiling, and they would think of something eventually; you weren't solving their problem for them!

The babysitting co-op we had with friends helped with their social development, as well as going on plenty of Marriage Prep weekends when they were small. Before long, we needed to make choices about their schooling—some of which we might well make differently if we could go back, knowing what we know now. We didn't do a lot of travel with them, although there were a couple trips to California to visit friends and relatives, and I remember one camping trip with my sister and sister-in-law and her daughter, their cousin. We had friends who were very generous about sharing their cabin at the lake, and those were some memorable times. All of these choices, although we were usually quite unaware of it at the time, were weaving not only our lives as a couple, but those of our family and the beginnings of each of their individual lives.

❖ ❖ ❖

We had decided that one of us would be home with the kids, rather than having other caregivers for them while we were working, which meant plenty of juggling of jobs during those years. You were writing more and more at this point—mainly articles but also some books, often in my parents' basement for some peace and quiet—while I was at first only teaching one evening class and then later more classes during the day at Gonzaga. It was a real risk, I suppose, for you to be trying to make a living as a freelance writer, and yet you were doing all right, and through the next number of years we both had a variety of jobs, which more or less allowed us to "keep the wolf from the door," as they say, but it also didn't mean we ever had much extra besides what we really needed.

As I mentioned earlier, whenever one of us has taken a "real job," with a more decent salary and actual benefits and all, it often doesn't work out all that well because God seems to have other plans for us. But when it comes to jobs or other choices, large or small, the best direction is almost never completely clear at the time, and each decision often doesn't seem like a big deal by itself.

❖ ❖ ❖

It may seem like a stretch to talk about the choices that we made on how to discipline or what to eat as being part of our spirituality, but they really were and are. Usually, we have weighed our options as best we could, added a little prayer at times, and made a choice, going where we seem to be led, trying to have a greater openness to love.

All of us are confronted with a constant process of making the best choices we can with the information and the values that we have and hoping that those decisions will continue to create and to weave our lives the best we can. You put the daily choice for love in our lives this way:

> I keep wanting to say over and over from the depths of my heart, I love you, love you so. But I'm beginning to realize that the only way I will ever be able to say it even adequately is by *living* for you, getting up in the morning, knocking myself out for you; walking and breathing and talking and singing and laughing and crying for you. . . eating and sleeping, seeking and finding for you. I love you, I will love you, I will *live* for you.

DYING AND RISING

When we promised for better or for worse in living for each other all those years ago, just like every other couple we had no idea what we were signing on for. Although there have been some experiences that were worse than we could have imagined, we also haven't seen the degree of challenges that some couples have. Even so, we seem to have had plenty to deal with at times.

In each situation, our faith has definitely helped—not only in knowing that God was there with us through whatever it was but also because of the Christian understanding of dying and rising, the paschal mystery. There has definitely been some dying and also rising from it in our lives together.

One of our hardest experiences was also one of the earliest. When we had been married a couple years and were living in Milwaukee, with you in grad school and me working in a parish there, we found out that we were pregnant. Although it had been our plan to wait to start a family until after you were finished with studies, once we began to wrap our heads around this incredible news, we were getting more and more excited about the prospect of being parents. I had just been given a baby shower at the parish where I was working and had ended the school year there when, in the middle of the night, my waters broke.

However, I was only a little more than five months along, and so we had a problem. We rushed to the hospital closest to where we lived—not the one where we had just begun prepared childbirth classes—and although they tried to revive our child, his lungs were not developed enough to allow him the ability to breathe on his own. (We had already chosen names and knew that his name was to be Brendan if it was a boy.) I went home with you the next day, but I didn't want to stay in the apartment and rest, as I was told to, while you went to your job, and so I had you drop me off at a park on the way.

I spent that day basically yelling and screaming at God about the unfairness of what had happened to us and how we were going to be good parents and that this wasn't okay. When I had finally exhausted my anger at God, I heard God's voice, I guess: "I want this child to be with me now more than to be with you." These words were quite comforting, allowing me and us to get through the turmoil of the next couple weeks as we decided that we missed the Northwest and wanted to head back there and see what might await us.

In the years since, the pain has of that loss has mostly healed, and I have asked Brendan at times to take care of his younger brothers when they needed it. At one point I even experienced his presence in a dream as a young adult, assuring me that all would be well with the other guys. But where was there any new life at all in the midst of such pain? Among other things, the loss of a child has given us far more empathy than we would have had otherwise for others in that situation, and I've been able to assure people many times that giving God their anger, like I did, can be an authentic and deeply honest kind of prayer.

❖ ❖ ❖

Many of our dyings and risings have been far smaller than that—sometimes so small that they hardly seem to "qualify," but in some ways they are harder to identify as dying and rising because of their being more minor.

There was the time, for example, when I had decided to try to do further graduate studies myself, to get a PhD, and we went back to Toronto to check out the situation, since that looked like the most promising program to which I had been accepted. (The challenge at that point was that all three of our sons were in grade school, so we had to find a realistic place for them while I took several years to finish the degree.) As we checked out the specifics in Toronto, it became clearer and clearer that, although the studies would have been very good for my needs, it just wouldn't have worked out for our family or for our finances.

So, for me, there was a dying that happened as we left Toronto, knowing that my career needed to be sacrificed for the family's sake. A couple of the "risings" in this for me—that I can see now but couldn't at the time—are that my focus has been more pastoral and applied and less academic than it would have been otherwise and also that our family was able to have the stable support system we had already developed here by then.

A little later, several challenges "collided," and we weren't sure at the time what was going to happen. I had decided that, in order to stay in Spokane and work with families, the best way for me was to get a degree in counseling, so I was studying that topic and wasn't working when we found another house across town that was bigger and nicer for our growing family. We thought we had a firm buyer for our old house as we made an offer on the new one, but the other deal fell through, and we ended up owning two houses until we could sell the first one! I still don't know how we did it then. The house we bought at that time has been such a wonderful home for us and a place of welcome and refuge that, even though it was hard at the time, it has been a source of new life for us.

So many of these situations of dying and rising rested on us relying on each other. You talked about that dynamic very early in our relationship:

> I need you so; and what and where is "I" if I give it all to you?
> Dependence upon each other becomes standing on our own

four feet . . . a man leaves his mother and gives himself to his wife and two become as one flesh, one sacrament, one divine promise—and promises to keep. . . and miles to go . . . and *God* will be all in all . . . and death and resurrection . . . and life depends on us, and without us there will be no meaning; there will be only two "I"s smiling bravely alone.

❖ ❖ ❖

Most of the hardest "deaths" have not just involved the two of us but our children as well. Recently I have realized that each of our sons has had quite a serious challenge to confront in their lives, which also involved the whole family. In recent years our oldest son has had to deal with lymphoma, which seemed to pop up fairly quickly, although he knew something wasn't right for a while before. Thankfully, with quick detection and aggressive chemo treatment, as well as great support from his wife and his workplace, he was cancer-free within six months, but with a whole new appreciation for the gift that his life is.

Our second son was in a serious car accident years ago that left him with some significant head injuries and a week in the hospital, much of it in intensive care. Thanks to excellent medical care and a resilient adolescent body, he was back playing basketball within a month or two. But he has had to deal with some of the more subtle long-term issues that can result from head injuries. Once again, the support of others in prayer was a big part of what pulled us through that experience.

The youngest of our three sons has had the hardest challenge of all of us, without question. He has been battling paranoid schizophrenia since his teens and is one of the most talented artists and thoughtful people we know. It was so heartbreaking to watch the illness rob him of his sense of perspective and turn him potentially dangerous a time or two. There were many years when we tried unsuccessfully to get him the help he so badly needed and even had to evict him from our home at one point.

He is now living on his own, healthy and doing well—with the medication he needs. And we are able to help him when he needs it. But there were definitely times when it was hard to see the possibility of any new life, any rising, from the nightmare that we were watching unfold. Now we can see that we would never have fully understood what a heartbreak mental illness can be for the whole family without experiencing it ourselves, and now we all know that our love can handle even this kind of challenge with the right boundaries and proper resources.

❖ ❖ ❖

There have certainly been other times of dying and rising in our lives—in a sense it's even a daily experience each day when we go to sleep and wake again. Gary Thomas, in his book *Sacred Marriage*, says that we can't choose what trials we face, just like we can't choose our physical aches. Like others our ages, we've had to face the deaths of our parents and grandparents along the way and differences in the way various family members grieve those losses. There have also been some health issues for us both, including the summer when I broke my ankle in a bike accident and had to ask for help for a long time just to get around. Most, but not all, of our surgeries have been minor ones, and who knows what lies ahead for us, which is what I'll consider next.

Whatever we have had to face, or may have to face in the future, we have always had our love for each other, strong enough to sustain us through anything that may come along. Here's how you put it all those years ago:

> Something I am discerning is the power your love gives me to be free mentally, emotionally, spiritually, from the pressure and stress times. I just think of what we have been given, of the fact of us, of how much I love you, need you, embrace you in my heart and soul, and I can't help but distance myself from becoming more concerned than I should be about a particular rough spot.

We've had our "rough spots," indeed, as every couple has, but our love and the awareness of dying and rising has made all the difference in getting through those times, stronger for having been tested and strengthened in the process.

WHAT LIES AHEAD

Allow me one last excerpt from your letters, Mitch, so many years ago:

> . . . I am becoming more convinced all the time that there is a Will at work in us that we simply may not in our right minds ignore. It could be that much more is at stake here than we may suspect . . . only the future will tell about that.

And here we are in that future. I don't really know that I thought about how long "till death do us part" might be and what we and our lives would look like this long after our wedding day. Looking ahead is always a risky business, but there are some components of what is up ahead for us that are, if not certain, at least likely and that I'd like to reflect on a bit here.

We're already at the point of retirement—you more than me so far—and that's been a good experience overall; we haven't been blessed with grandchildren to this point, as some of our friends have, but we've found other activities to keep us busy. Chances are good in the fairly near future that one or both of us will have to contend with more significant health issues than the usual aches and pains we are already experience. And, although I certainly hope it's no time soon, at some point one of us will probably need to cope with the loss of the other and how to go on alone.

We have had more time together in the past few years than we've had for most of our lives, with so much of our energy going toward work and kids in our earlier years. I've noticed that, although we've always encouraged each other to take time for ourselves, we now spend a good part of our days in separate spaces and activities, you upstairs in your office and banjo practice area, which used to be one of the kids' bedrooms, and me at my computer and writing space, sometimes correcting student papers or planning some new project. You do volunteer work one morning a week, and I'm still doing some teaching and other work, such as with engaged couples. It's been a good drawing apart, which allows the time we spend together to be just that much more special and giving us the space for our individual pursuits. We still go out for a date night, but on many other nights we'll also watch films on video at home. You've taken over more of the household duties as you're spending more time here, like making the bed and doing the pans, for which I'm really grateful.

We both know that physical frailty is ahead at some point, which is not an easy prospect but one which we can get through with the strength we've seen in the past and with many friends and our faith. We've watched some of people close to us face really difficult challenges, especially several friends and relatives caring for their spouses as Alzheimers or other dementia issues slowly took them away, which I think must be the hardest of all. You have been told that you have Parkinson's disease, at a very early and minor stage so far, and we're hoping that it won't advance much or at least very quickly, but we don't know what lies ahead with that. The dying and rising that we've already experienced gives us confidence for what the future may bring. Fr. Karl Rahner, the theologian I mentioned earlier, talks about how these experiences are "dying in installments," preparing us for the time that we finally let go.

And, speaking of a subject that we so rarely discuss in our culture, death, I used to wonder occasionally when you had to leave for a trip whether—God forbid—if you didn't come back, I could manage on my own. I certainly didn't want anything to happen to you—quite the opposite; I just realized that our lives were so completely interwoven that I wanted to make sure that I could cope if I had to without you. Hopefully, it will be a good long time before either of us hits that point, but at some point we will.

When that happens, hopefully all of what we have built together will help sustain us then. We have been strengthened by each other in every way I can think of, and we have a legacy of memories, as all couples do. We also have had plenty of opportunities in print and in speaking engagements to remind others about the holiness of what lies right before them, carefully hidden in the ordinary details of our lives. Each time we have had the opportunity to tell others about that, I believe it's God's sneaky way of trying to remind us of how much the holy *is* in the ordinary, right before us, which is why it's so easy to miss.

❖ ❖ ❖

Forty years ago, God began an experiment with the two of us, an experiment of freely-given and overwhelming grace, of a vocation toward the unknown, one which involved a community of family and friends, a subtle asceticism calling for forgetting self daily, one that was incarnational and holistic and about bodies as well as minds and souls, one that called for careful discernment and listening when it came to the choices we made, with plenty of dying and rising woven into the events of a life shared closely. Although that experiment has had its unique elements, it's not unlike the journey that couples everywhere are making, often only vaguely aware of the holiness of what lies right before them.

Thank you more than I can say, Mitch, for being a part of that experiment with me, of taking that amazing journey. Here's to many more years—together—in a love that continues to draw us closer to each other and, in the process, closer to the God of Love!

www.ingramcontent.com/pod-product-compliance
Lightning Source LLC
Chambersburg PA
CBHW070501090426
42735CB00012B/2648